GALILEO

A Gombay

Toronto July 1974

GALILEO

A Philosophical Study

DUDLEY SHAPERE

The University of Chicago Press
Chicago and London

DUDLEY SHAPERE is professor of philosophy and chairman of the Program in History and Philosophy of Science at the University of Illinois. He is the author of *Philosophical Problems of Natural Science.*
[1974]

The University of Chicago Press, Chicago 60637
The University of Chicago Press, Ltd., London

International Standard Book Number: 0–226–75005–1 (cloth)
Library of Congress Catalog Card Number: 73–92023

To Alfred and Catherine

Contents

Preface

The problem of the nature of the world in which we live, and the problem of how we are able to find out about that world, or at least are able to make rationally warranted claims about it, have always been at the heart of philosophy. Since the seventeenth century, however, there has been, under the name of "science," a reasonably steady and continuous growth of that knowledge and our methods of obtaining it. Whether or not there are kinds of knowledge other than scientific is perhaps only a matter of the breadth of definition we are willing to allow that term; but that science and its methods constitute a paradigm case of knowledge and the knowledge-acquiring process should be beyond dispute. It follows that an investigation of the character of the knowledge-claims of science, and of the methods by which those knowledge-claims are justified, is of fundamental importance to philosophy. The importance of an understanding of science also follows from the central role that subject has played, and continues to play, in modern civilization.

Despite the long and increasing success of science, despite the efforts lavished on its analysis, and despite the vast amount of material uncovered in this century regarding its development, there is still little agreement as to what it claims to be accomplishing or how it manages to accomplish it. In recent years controversy has arisen over interpretations which seem to leave it, and human knowledge generally, a matter of subjective opinion, transitory fad, or cultural dogma, so that the claim that science achieves "knowledge" appears gratuitous at best. Yet the more traditional kind of interpretation seems to make science a drudgery, a mindless gathering of facts and a mechanical calculating of further results on the basis of those facts—an interpretation which seems to leave little or no room for creative imagination, as the newer view, described above, seems to make it nothing else. The traditional approach is far from dead: it is still reflected in the way science is taught, and in the view that it is utterly irrelevant to the "humanistic" disciplines, and in the related view that it is a Frankenstein monster which, if not rigidly controlled, constitutes a menace to rather than an integral part of civilization.

The present work is the first of a projected series of detailed studies, by the present author, of important episodes in the development of science—studies which, while aiming at being as historically and scientifically responsible as the subject-matter and the capacities of the author allow, will focus on those facets of the selected episodes which are of relevance to the philosophical questions concerning the rationale of the scientific enterprise. In connection with this primary aim, the studies will involve an attempt not only to give coherent interpretations of the cases, and ultimately to extract any available generalizations and systematizations from those cases, but also to provide critical analyses of interpretations of the cases by philosophers and historians: to put philosophical theses about science to the tests of conceptual analysis and historical record, and to show how the historian's (and the scientist's) interpretations of the historical record are frequently distorted by conceptual presuppositions or confusions.

Finally, the series will examine the extent to which problems of science and philosophy are intertwined, both in their historical development and their systematic relations. Thus, it will examine the extent of interaction between science and at least one humanistic discipline (but a very fundamental one). It is thus hoped that, while not sacrificing depth and responsibility of analysis, the studies will be relevant and accessible not only to philosophers and historians of science, but to scientists and humanists as well.

This book does not claim complete coverage of all of Galileo's work and that of his predecessors, or of the vast secondary literature on these topics. Nor does it claim that no episodes other than those discussed here contributed significantly to the scientific revolution. But the episode chosen here was an important one, and its importance is increased by the fact that it has been used to support a variety of interpretations of the nature of science.

It is impossible to thank all those who have contributed to my thinking about the topics of this book; perhaps I can single out D. Bantz, L. Darden, H. Hardgrave, and W. R. Shea. But I cannot omit mentioning the probing questions of many students in the lectures on which much of this book is based. I also thank the staff of the University of Chicago Press for their valuable help and suggestions in the final preparation of the book, and the National Science Foundation for its support of my research on the rationale of scientific development.

GALILEO

1

Galileo and the Interpretation of Science

That Galileo was a major figure in the history of science can hardly be doubted. He was at least an important, and possibly the dominant, figure in what has come to be called the scientific revolution of the seventeenth century—a historical episode which, far from being restricted to science in its implications, has had the most profound influence in shaping the character of modern civilization as a whole.

The nature of Galileo's contribution was once believed to be perfectly clear and straightforward. According to that interpretation, thought about the nature of the world before Galileo was rooted either in blind superstition, unquestioning acceptance of authority, or ill-founded speculation masking itself under the name of "Reason." Galileo, breaking completely with the past, is alleged to have invented a new method of obtaining knowledge, the *empirical* or *experimental* or *scientific* method, and, by employing it, without any preconceptions or prejudices whatever, to have elicited from his observations some of nature's deepest secrets. Most important (but by no means all) of these, obtained primarily from observations and experiments with the inclined plane, the pendulum, and the telescope, were the following:

1. the Principle of Inertia—that every body continues in a state of rest or uniform rectilinear motion forever unless acted upon by an external force—a principle which became the cornerstone of Newtonian science;
2. the laws of falling bodies, which, in modern form, are: $s = \frac{1}{2}at^2$; $v = at$; $v = (2as)^{\frac{1}{2}}$ (where s is the distance

3

fallen, t the time of fall, v the velocity, and a the constant of acceleration); in particular—as revealed by
the absence in these formulas of any reference to the
mass or other specific characteristics of the falling
bodies—he found that the rate of fall is independent
of the constitution of the falling body: all bodies fall
at the same rate, at least in a vacuum;

3. the fact that the path of a projectile is a parabola;
4. numerous astronomical discoveries establishing the
   Copernican system of astronomy, which held that the
   earth, far from being the center of the universe, is
   merely one of the planets, all of which revolve around
   the sun.

The most famous proponent of this kind of interpretation
was the nineteenth-century Austrian philosopher-scientist
Ernst Mach, who, in his classic and highly influential work,
The Science of Mechanics, analyzed Galileo's work in considerable detail, arguing that "dynamics . . . is an entirely
new science" (Mach, 151) invented by Galileo. With respect
to the behavior of falling bodies, for example, "no part of
the knowledge and ideas on this subject with which we are
now so familiar existed in Galileo's time, but . . . Galileo
had to create these ideas and means for us" (Mach, 159).
Galileo "did not supply us with a *theory* of the falling of
bodies, but investigated and established, wholly without
preformed opinions, the *actual facts* of falling" (Mach, 167;
here and elsewhere, italics are his). Galileo's technique was
one of "gradually *adapting* . . . his thoughts to the facts"
(Mach, 167), and "an entirely new notion to which Galileo
was led [by those facts] is the idea of *acceleration*" (Mach,
174). "That it is *accelerations* which are the immediate
effects of the circumstances that determine motion, that is,
of the forces, is a fact which Galileo *perceived* in the natural phenomena" (Mach, 171). He was thus able to arrive at
his results only when (in his mature period) he "investigated the motion of falling experimentally and without taking its causes into consideration" (Mach, 189)—that is,
when he "dropped the question as to the 'why' and inquired
the 'how' of the many motions which can be observed"
(Mach, 155). In the case of the Principle of Inertia, Mach

reconstructs Galileo's thought as follows. A body, after rolling down the inclined plane *AB*, will (neglecting friction

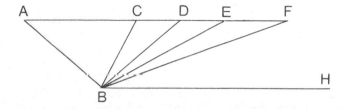

and air resistance) ascend another plane (for example, *BC*, *BD*, etc.) to the height from which it was originally released—that is, to the line *AF*, decelerating as it rises. "The nearer the planes *BC*, *BD*, *BE*, *BF* approach to the horizontal plane *BH*, the less will the retardation of the body on those planes be, and the longer and further will it move on them. On the horizontal plane *BH* the retardation vanishes *entirely* . . . and the body will continue to move infinitely long and infinitely far with *constant* velocity. Thus advancing to the limiting case of the problem presented, Galileo discovers the so-called law of inertia" (Mach, 168–69). Once possessing this law, Mach claims, Galileo was able to derive the parabolic path of a projectile as a combination of a uniform horizontal motion and an accelerated motion of falling.

Thus, by a procedure of "isolating and emphasizing what is deemed of importance, by neglecting what is subsidiary, by *abstracting*, by idealizing" (Mach, 161), by experimenting and passing to a "limiting case of the problem presented," Galileo's work is not merely historically interesting; it also provides an instructive model of proper scientific procedure. In general, Mach contends, science must begin with such idealized situations and perform experiments on them; and

> Once we have reached a theory that applies to a particular case, we proceed gradually to modify in thought the conditions of that case, as far as it is at all possible, and endeavor in so doing to adhere throughout as closely as we can to the conception originally reached. There is no method of procedure more surely calculated to lead to

that comprehension of all natural phenomena which is the *simplest* and also attainable with the least expenditure of mentality and feeling. (Mach, 168)

According to Mach, this is not merely the procedure that Galileo *did* use in achieving his results; it is also the kind of procedure that he, and all good scientists, *ought* to adopt.

In emphasizing the observational and experimental aspects of Galileo's work, Mach can fairly be accused of failing to give proper weight to the importance of Galileo's mathematical approach to the study of nature. That aspect, it may be (and has been) claimed, is at least as important in the development of modern science as the empirical side, and a more balanced view than Mach's would give due recognition to the role of both experiment and mathematics. Indeed, we will find writers on Galileo who say that the mathematical is the most important aspect; and even more surprisingly to those who have been brought up on the Machian interpretation, those writers sometimes go so far as to say that the empirical aspect was not even present in Galileo, or at least that it played a very minor role in the development of his thought. And more generally, according to those authors—most notably, Alexandre Koyré and his numerous followers—observation and experiment played no role, or at best played an insignificant one, in the birth of modern science. Koyré and his followers even take the argument one step further: the emphasis on mathematics at the expense of experiment implies, for them, that Galileo was, methodologically, a *rationalist*. And thus, according to Koyré, the scientific work of Galileo, and hence the beginning of modern science, far from being an empiricist reaction against dogmatic Aristotelianism, had its deepest roots in a revival of Platonism.

But we shall examine that interpretation in more detail later; for the present, let us return to Mach. The kind of interpretation he offers of Galileo's work is still widespread; most notably, it is found (sometimes supplemented by attention to the role of mathematics) almost universally in discussions of proper scientific method in physics texts, as the following examples will illustrate.

The work of Galileo is also important because it established a new method, a new direction for scientific investigations. A careful study of the methods he used will provide an illustration of the basic approach that has subsequently dominated the physical sciences. (J. A. Ripley, *The Elements and Structure of the Physical Sciences* [New York: Wiley, 1964], p. 90)

Galileo's contribution to present scientific thinking was threefold: (1) he was the first to appreciate the value of experiment and might well be called the father of experimental physics; (2) he was able to imagine an ideal situation, such as a frictionless medium, and thereby to explain discrepancies between actual and theoretical results; and (3) he recognized the value of mathematical analysis in the study of physical principles. (E. Hausmann and E. P. Slack, *Physics* [New York: Van Nostrand, 1957], p. 36)

It is generally admitted that the true spirit of modern scientific inquiry had its first clear expression in the work of the gifted Italian scientist Galileo Galilei. . . . Galileo's insistence on systematic observation and experimentation as the essential basis of scientific work is the outstanding characteristic of the science of today. It is often said that he replaced the question "Why?", which Aristotle put to nature, with "How?" (I. M. Freeman, *Physics: Principles and Insights* [New York: McGraw-Hill, 1968], p. 11)

Such examples could be repeated almost indefinitely. On the other hand, one had best not read too many physics texts; otherwise one might get contradictory reports about the nature of scientific method as illustrated by Galileo's work.

At the same time that the pioneer scientists [including Galileo] were trying to get an accurate description of different kinds of motion, they also wondered about the causes and origins of these motions. Not only the "how," but the "why" of motions was sought; for the two aspects of motion, description and cause, are linked to each other. (A. Marantz, *Physics* [New York: Benziger, 1969], p. 98)

Such views are also frequently found in the writings of professional historians of science. Nevertheless, even at the time Mach was writing, new historical information was being uncovered which led to serious criticisms of his interpretation, and ultimately to radically different interpretations, not only of Galileo's work, but also of the scientific revolution as a whole, and ultimately of the nature of science itself. (It is interesting to follow Mach through successive editions of his book as he tries to come to grips with that new information and the criticisms based on it, while at the same time maintaining substantially his original view.) In many respects, the story of those criticisms and new interpretations is the story of the development of the modern subject of the history of science, and constitutes as well the background of some of today's stormiest and most fundamental debates about the nature of science.

Beginning in 1881 the hitherto-unpublished *Notebooks* of Leonardo da Vinci began to appear. Leonardo was found to have had many of the same ideas as had previously been attributed to Galileo's originality. At first this coincidence was attributed to the universal genius of Leonardo; but soon those same ideas were found to have been the common property of a number of Galileo's immediate predecessors. Pierre Duhem therefore undertook a search for the roots of those ideas and, in a series of monumental works in the first years of the twentieth century, argued in effect that practically all the ideas attributed to Galileo had already been discovered in the fourteenth century, principally by the "Impetus Theorists" at the University of Paris, in the context of criticism and modification of Aristotle's philosophy—which in turn had arisen out of critical analysis of his predecessors. The work of Galileo, according to Duhem, did not mark a sharp and complete break with a rationalistic (or worse, perhaps, a superstitious) past; it was not a new creation, wholly independent of philosophy and rejecting it; on the contrary, science and philosophy developed together, inseparably, out of a common Greek and medieval heritage. And Galileo was not the creator of the scientific revolution, but, perhaps at best, an effective propagandist for what had essentially been accomplished over two centuries before.

The attempt to substantiate or refute Duhem's thesis has generated a vast amount of historical research and reinterpretation of Galileo and the scientific revolution, which in turn has produced a remarkable deepening of our understanding of scientific change. It has by no means, however, produced unanimous agreement about the character of the "scientific revolution" (if indeed it is still possible to speak of such an event), or about Galileo's role in the birth and development of modern science, or about the nature of the scientific enterprise itself. The purpose of this book will be to examine some crucial aspects of these issues and controversies.

We will not attempt anything like a complete treatment of these topics or, in particular, of the work of Galileo on which our discussion will center. We will deal primarily with Galileo's role in the development of mechanics (although we shall also consider the relation of some of his other work, especially astronomical, to his mechanics). And we shall focus our attention on two questions which will prove to be central to the issues which have just been discussed. The first concerns the role in his thought of the principle of inertia. There is much reason, as we will find, for saying that the arrival at this principle constituted the essence of the transition from Greek and medieval thought to the incontestably modern science of Newton's *Principia*. How was this transition brought about, and what was it about prior thought that required modification or abandonment in order to bring it about? Many writers (like Mach), following the testimony of Sir Isaac Newton himself, have attributed the discovery of the principle to Galileo; but we will find serious grounds for questioning that attribution. But if he did not have the principle, was he well on the way toward it? And if so, how far? And to the extent that he had not attained it, what, if anything, was characteristically new and "modern" in his thought?

This book will also examine a cluster of questions regarding the "method" by which Galileo arrived at his substantive conclusions. To what extent did he obtain his results by experiment? To what extent did he think he had so obtained them? To what extent did he think he *ought* to have

so obtained them? To what extent *could* he have so obtained them? (It will prove important for us to distinguish
these questions.) What methodological doctrines were involved in his use of mathematics, and, in particular, did
they involve a commitment to a form of Platonic rationalism and a rejection of the empiricism which traditional
interpretations, as typified by Mach, have attributed to him?
What, precisely, was the role of "idealization" and "thought
experiments" in his method, and to what extent was the use
of such techniques a unique feature of a new "scientific"
approach which Galileo was introducing? To what extent
did he dismiss questions about the "Why?" of motion and
concentrate only on the "How?"

In these investigations, we must take a keenly skeptical
attitude toward the central ideas in terms of which our
questions themselves are formulated. For one lesson of the
philosophy of science is that such concepts as *empirical* and
rational, to mention only two, cannot be employed un-
critically. There is a wide variety of very divergent views
calling themselves "empiricist," for example; and simply
distinguishing them is not sufficient for raising such questions as ours, because no one of those variant views is even
perfectly clear, and even to the extent to which it is, we
must still ask whether such a method even *could* be put
into practice. Thus in asking whether Galileo was an
"empiricist," we must not only distinguish the questions
raised in the preceding paragraph; we must also, for each
of those questions, determine as clearly as possible the
sense or senses in which he might have, or might have
thought he had, or might have thought he ought to have,
been an "empiricist." And, for the latter two of these alternatives, we must ask whether he *could* have arrived at his
results by such an "empirical" method that he might have
thought he had or ought to have employed. Similar care
must be taken with such terms as *observational*, *experimental*, and *theoretical*, for example. We shall find cases in
which interpretations offered by historians of science, for
all their conscientiousness about the historical facts, have
been vitiated by an inadequate sensitivity to such intricate
philosophical issues.

Similarly, the question about the place of "Why?" and "How?" in Galileo's thought must be approached with caution. Clearly, there are two different questions involved in asking about the "Why?" of motion. On the one hand, there is the question of the *cause* of motion, and on the other hand, that of the *purpose* of motion. Did Galileo, in his (mature) treatment of motion, dismiss the question "Why?" in both these senses? In either?

In attempting to understand Galileo's thoughts and methods, we will of course pay close attention to his own statements and arguments, not only with a view to reporting what he said, but also to evaluating the logical validity of his claims. But we shall also look at his work in the light of the intellectual background, revealed by Duhem and his successors, in terms of which, or against which, his own ideas were framed. We shall also examine critically some of the major interpretations of Galileo's thought and methods that have been proposed in recent years. And finally, we will consider some broader implications of our analysis: its relevance to a more general understanding of the nature of science, and particularly of scientific development and innovation.

Although this book is primarily concerned with Galileo's thought, it will be useful to survey briefly some of the pertinent facts of his life.[1] Galileo Galilei was born on 15 February 1564, at or near Pisa; his father, Vincenzio, was a musician. In 1581 Galileo entered the University of Pisa as a medical student; however, he soon turned his interests to mathematics. After three years, having failed to obtain a scholarship, Galileo left the university without having received his degree. He continued his mathematical studies, however, and wrote his first scientific paper, "The Little Balance," in which—significantly, as we shall see—he dealt with the question of how Archimedes might have discovered that King Hiero had been cheated by the goldsmith who made his crown. Galileo also showed in that treatise his talent for scientific instrumentation by describing the construction of a hydrostatic balance. During these years, he also worked out some theorems on centers of gravity of certain solids. This work stood him in good stead, for in 1589, through the influence of Marquis Guidobaldo del Monte, who had been impressed by it, he received an appointment in mathematics at the University of Pisa. It was here that he composed his first major (though unpublished) work, *On Motion*, which we will discuss in chapter 3.

Galileo was never one to shy away from controversy, and the talent for irony and sarcasm which we find in his works was by no means confined to his writing. This aspect of his personality seems to have gained him some enemies at Pisa, and in 1592 he resigned his post there, having in the meantime, again with Guidobaldo's help, secured a position in mathematics at the University of Padua, then one of the greatest centers of learning in the world. Here over the next eighteen years his ideas on mechanics gradually developed, leaving behind many of the views expressed in *On Motion*, until by the time he left Padua in 1610 he had substantially completed the material that would, much later, be incorporated into the *Discourses and Mathematical Demonstrations Concerning Two New Sciences Pertaining to Mechanics and Local Motions* (customarily referred to as the *Two New Sciences*, or simply as the *Discourses*). This material comprises the last section of the First Day and the entirety of the Third Day of that work.

At Padua, too, he found a congenial intellectual and social atmosphere and made many friends, including Giovanfrancesco Sagredo, a Venetian nobleman, whose name was later given to one of the participants in the *Dialogue Concerning the Two Chief World Systems* and the *Two New Sciences*. In those works, Sagredo is given the character of the intelligent, open-minded intermediary between the defenders of the two opposing views: Simplicio, the disciple of Aristotle (whose name not only carries the all-too-obvious connotation, but also is reminiscent of the great sixth-century commentator on Aristotle, Simplicius); and Salviati, who is clearly the spokesman of Galileo. (It should come as no surprise that the open-minded Sagredo invariably comes down on the side of Salviati.) Salviati also derives his name from a friend of Galileo's, the Florentine Filippo Salviati.

For over ten years of his stay in Padua Galileo had a mistress, Marina Gamba, who bore him two daughters and a son. When Galileo left Padua, they separated, apparently on good terms, she remaining behind and marrying shortly after his departure.

During these years Galileo became acquainted with the work of artisans in the vicinity. He himself constructed a device for measuring temperature and a form of compass which was of great utility in certain calculations. His notes of the period contain references to the pendulum and to the behavior of bodies on inclined planes; we shall consider later whether these references imply that he actually performed experiments. He gave courses on the Ptolemaic system of astronomy, though without criticizing the doctrine; he does not even discuss it in his elementary *Treatise on the Sphere, or Cosmography* (1597), mentioning it only twice in passing. In that same year, however, he wrote two letters suggesting that he was at least willing to defend the rival Copernican system, and perhaps had even adopted it privately. In the first he defended Copernicanism against a specific objection that had recently been raised. The other was an acknowledgment of receipt of a copy of Johannes Kepler's *Mysterium Cosmographicum*; having had time only to glance at the preface, Galileo wrote Kepler that

> I have for many years past subscribed to the teaching of Copernicus, and from it I have been able to demonstrate causes of many phenomena which without doubt cannot be explained by the traditional hypothesis. I have worked out proofs, as well as computations of contrary arguments which, however, I thus far did not dare to make publicly known, being frightened by the fate of our master Copernicus who, though having gained immortal fame in the eyes of a few, has been ridiculed and exploded by innumerable others—for so great is the number of fools. I should indeed venture to disclose my opinion, if there were more men like you; since there are none, I shall desist from such a task.

In spite of these declarations, any such "proofs" have not survived, and there is little positive evidence, apart from these letters, that he was committed at this time, or at any time before 1610, to the Copernican theory. If he was, he certainly could not have been "frightened" (as if Galileo ever was, except perhaps when, nearly seventy years old, he faced the Inquisition) by fear of persecution; and on other occasions he never shrank from the possibility of ridicule; why should he have hesitated to make his convictions known on this occasion? It seems much more likely that, although he was thinking about these astronomical matters during his Paduan period, and had perhaps devised arguments which could support Copernicanism (perhaps some, like his theory of the tides, which were later incorporated into the *Two Chief World Systems*), he had not at this time made up his mind. Perhaps he was moving more and more in the direction of Copernicanism, accumulating new arguments in its favor. For instance, in 1604 a new star or nova appeared in the sky, and Galileo gave a series of three public lectures on the subject. Although only part of the text of his lectures has survived, he apparently argued that the nova provided a strong argument for Copernicanism. Nevertheless, there seems little support for the view, advanced by some, that, at least before 1610, his interest in mechanics was fostered by an aim to provide a physical basis for Copernican astronomy. (Such a view would make the "scientific revolution" a revolution fundamentally in astronomy rather than in mechanics—a Copernican rather than a Galilean revolution.)

The situation changed radically in 1609, when he heard about an instrument constructed by a Dutchman which could make distant objects appear nearer. With no more information than this, Galileo constructed such an instrument—a telescope—for himself, and by early the following year had made an improved version of about thirty power. Using this instrument to observe the heavens, Galileo discovered that the Milky Way consists of innumerable stars, that the Moon has mountains and other surface features, and that Jupiter has four satellites, thus serving as a miniature model of a Copernican system. In March 1610 he published these results in a book, *The Starry Messenger*. Subsequently he discovered the phases of Venus; the "handles" —or perhaps they were satellites—of Saturn, later found to be rings around the planet; and the spots on the sun whose positional changes indicated to him that the sun rotates on an axis. Whether or not he had been an adherent of Copernicanism before, all these discoveries certainly confirmed him in that belief. Having named the satellites of Jupiter the "Medician Stars," he was rewarded for this compliment by the Grand Duke of Florence by an appointment as his Chief Mathematician and Philosopher. Galileo resigned his position at Padua and moved to Florence. It was to prove an unfortunate move. His friend Sagredo strongly urged him not to make it, for he was leaving the free atmosphere of the Venetian Republic to live in the shadow of the intrigue of the Medici court and the authority of the Church.

Galileo's astronomical discoveries, and the Copernicanism which he based on them, as well as his increasingly vocal criticism of Aristotelianism in general, aroused considerable opposition; and there were also the disputes over priority of discovery which were so common in those days. Over the next several years, he was involved in numerous controversies which bore fruit in equally numerous publications. The most important of these were the following:

Discourse on Bodies Placed in Water (1612), in which he defended Archimedes' view of floating bodies against Aristotle. It is noteworthy that, in a discussion of this subject at the home of the Grand Duke, one of the participants was Cardinal Maffeo Barberini, later to become Pope Urban VIII. Barberini took Galileo's side in the debate.

Letters on Sunspots (1613), in which he argued that the spots were actually surface features of the sun, and not, for example, small planets. Further, he maintained, since they appeared and disappeared at irregular intervals, they counted against the Aristotelian contention that no such changes could occur in the heavens.

The Assayer (1623), a work which arose as a consequence of a bitter and protracted dispute over the nature of comets. In 1619 Father Orazio Grassi, a Jesuit, had published a work defending Tycho Brahe's view that comets exist beyond the moon. (By measurements of parallax—the angular shift in position of a body against its background when it is viewed from different places, e.g., on the earth's surface—Tycho and others had determined that these parallactic shifts of comets are too small for them to be sublunar.)

Galileo replied in the *Discourse on the Comets*, which he published under the name of one of his disciples, Mario Guiducci. While agreeing with Aristotle that comets are "exhalations" rising from the earth, he did not agree that their visibility is a result of their having caught fire in the upper reaches of the sublunar realm. Rather, having risen (in straight lines), they become visible by refracting the light of the sun; thus they are "mere appearances, reflections of light, images, and wandering simulacra" (Guiducci, *Discourse on the Comets*, p. 36). And as to the Tychonic view,

> if parallax has no cogency in determining the distances of all these refractions or reflections, images, appearances, and illusions because they change place as the observer moves (and change not only their places but their identities), I shall not believe that parallax has really any place in [the measurement of distances of] comets until it is first proved that comets are not reflections of light, but are unique, fixed, real, and permanent objects. (Guiducci, p. 39)

Grassi, now writing under the pseudonym Lothario Sarsi Sigensano, replied immediately, pointing out a number of obvious flaws in Galileo's arguments. Galileo's response to this attack was *The Assayer*, a polemical masterpiece in which he defended his previous position, expanded, with brutal sarcasm, his attack on Tycho and his system of astronomy, and commented rather extensively on the nature and methods of science.

Even before the controversy on comets, Galileo had begun to find himself involved in disputes about the relation of his astronomical views to religion. In a letter to a disciple, Benedetto Castelli, Galileo had maintained that the language of the Bible, being subject to various interpretations, should not be used to judge scientific results except as a last resort. This letter fell into the hands of certain Dominicans, and a secret inquiry was initiated. The proceedings went rather slowly, and much of the testimony was favorable to Galileo; he himself, meanwhile, attempted a careful restatement of his views in a *Letter to the Grand Duchess Christina* (1615).

However, the inquiry became involved in a wider struggle between conservatives, largely members of the Dominican order, and liberals, mainly Jesuits, in the Church. The latter group favored an open-minded attitude toward new ideas, and were generally favorable to Galileo's cause; however, in the end they failed to act strongly in his behalf. Two propositions were denounced, the first as foolish, the second as erroneous:

> That the sun is the center of the universe, and consequently is not moved by any local motion.
> That the earth is not the center of the universe nor is it motionless, but moves as a whole, and also with the diurnal motion [i.e., daily rotation on its axis as well as annual revolution around the sun].

In March 1616, Copernicus' *On the Revolution of the Heavenly Spheres* and Didacus Astunica's *Commentary on Job* were "suspended" until corrected; one book, and one only, by Paolo Antonio Foscarini, was condemned outright. Galileo's own astronomical writings were not listed. But he was called before Cardinal Robert Bellarmine and the Father Commissary General of the Holy Office, and, at least according to the memorandum of the meeting, was instructed to abstain from holding, teaching, or defending Copernicanism. The memorandum records that he promised to obey the injunction.

It is impossible to enter here into the controversies regarding the authenticity of this memorandum, which was to serve as the basis of Galileo's trial in 1633, seventeen years later. It is certain that it was written in 1616, and so is not a later forgery; but there are many grounds for suspecting that it does not record faithfully what happened in the confrontation. It was not signed by those present (or alleged to have been present), so that, authentic or not, its official status was in doubt. At the time some interpreted the whole episode as, if not a triumph, at least not an out-and-out defeat for the liberal "modernists": after all, the two propositions denounced were not direct quotations from any works; they were not declared flatly heretical; and Galileo's own treatment could be looked upon as being exceptionally mild. Galileo himself, whether sincerely or not, expressed the view that the judgment was a minor victory. Further, he was even granted a "most benign" audience with the pope; and Bellarmine himself, at Galileo's request, presented him with a document declaring that:

> We, Robert Cardinal Bellarmine, having heard that Signor Galileo Galilei is calumniated or imputed to have abjured in our hand, and even of having been given salutary penance for this; and inquiries having been made as to the truth, we say that the said Signor Galilei has not abjured any opinion or doctrine of his in our hand nor in that of anyone else at Rome, much less anywhere else, to our knowledge; nor has he received penance of any sort; but he has only been told the decision made by His Holiness and published by the Holy Congregation of the Index, in which it is declared that the doctrine attributed to Copernicus, that the earth moves round the sun and that the sun is fixed in the center of the universe without moving from west to east, is contrary to the Holy Scriptures, and therefore cannot be defended or held. And in witness of this we have written and signed this with our own hand.

No doubt these ambiguities reflected the deep internal struggles in the Church itself; but in any case, they could not but have made a man of Galileo's temperament feel that the injunctions were not to be taken too seriously.

In 1623, Maffeo Barberini, who as we saw above had sided with Galileo in a debate on floating bodies, and had even written the poem praising Galileo's telescopic discoveries, became Pope Urban VIII; Galileo's *Assayer*, published that year, was dedicated to him. Presumably feeling that he now had powerful protection, Galileo concentrated his efforts during the following few years on a long-planned work on astronomy. This book, the *Dialogue Concerning the Two Chief World Systems*, was finally completed in 1630. Galileo took the manuscript to Rome for official licensing and, after much delay and argument, the book was approved by the Church authorities and was published in 1632.

In his preface, Galileo professed that

I have taken the Copernican side in the discourse, proceeding as with a pure mathematical hypothesis and striving by every artifice to represent it as superior to supposing the earth motionless—not, indeed, absolutely, but as against the arguments of some professed Peripatetics [i.e., Aristotelians]. (*Two Chief World Systems*, p. 6)

And again, in the final pages, he has Salviati declare that

I do not claim and have not claimed from others that assent which I myself do not give to this invention [i.e., Copernicanism], which may very easily turn out to be a most foolish hallucination and a majestic paradox. (p. 463)

Yet these protestations seem limp, and even perhaps insolent, when compared with the overwhelming weight of arguments for Copernicanism in the text itself—ingenious and powerful even when incorrect from the standpoint of later science. No reader could believe, then or now, that Galileo had obeyed the injunction—that he had not advocated Copernicanism, much less treated it as a mere "mathematical hypothesis." And Simplicio, the defender of Aristotle and therefore of tradition, was made to appear a fool. The Church authorities, needless to say, were incensed. Far worse: for on the closing page, Simplicio declares that, despite the ingenuity of Salviati's arguments, he does not consider them true and conclusive, because of "a most solid doctrine that I once heard from a most eminent and learned person." The argument was to the effect that, though appearances might make it seem that the earth goes around the sun, God might have so constructed things that those very appearances are produced by the sun going around the earth. Coming at the end of so powerful a book, such an argument —and the "eminent and learned person" who originated it— must appear simplistic indeed! Unfortunately, that person was no less than Urban himself. It seemed to him—and others were willing to let him be convinced—that Galileo was mocking him, and perhaps intended Simplicio to be a caricature of him. Other events, too, conspired to doom Galileo. Father Riccardi, the man who issued the authorization for publication, was a Dominican; and it is possible that the Jesuits, no longer sympathetic to Galileo in any case, saw in this indiscretion an opportunity to humiliate the rival order. On a larger scale, the political struggle between France and Spain over control of Italy became a factor: Urban owed his election as pope to the cardinals favoring the French; Galileo's mentor, the Grand Duke, allied himself with the Spanish. However, the Grand Duke weakly backed away from a possible conflict with the pope, and failed to support Galileo. Under such circumstances, the outcome was inevitable: Galileo was brought before the Inquisition for trial. The authorization he had obtained for publication was explained away, and itself converted into a crime: in seeking such approval, Galileo had violated the injunction given him by Bellarmine in 1616; and he had deceived Riccardi by not informing him of that injunction. The prosecution had difficulties because of the questionable character of the minute reporting Bellarmine's injunction, and even more because of the signed note Galileo had obtained from Bellarmine; and so their line of questioning was designed to elicit from Galileo an admission that some such injunction or "precept" had been issued. Galileo fell into the trap: he unguardedly used the word *precept*. The questioning intensified, and Galileo claimed that the reason he had not felt the need to inform Riccardi of the "precept" was that the *Dialogue*, far from violating that precept by advocating Copernicanism, was written to show that the arguments for it were "invalid and inconclusive." Naturally, it was easy then to force him to admit that many sections in the book did present Copernicanism in an extremely favorable light. Under rigorous examination (but certainly not under torture), the old man confessed that "I do not hold nor have I held to this opinion of Copernicus since the precept was given to me that I must abandon it." The sentence was that the *Dialogue* be banned and Galileo condemned to life imprisonment. The latter part, however, was commuted: he was allowed to remain in his own villa near Florence to the end of his life. He was also forbidden to publish further.

During the following years, he again returned to his studies of mechanics, and completed his great *Discourses and Mathematical Demonstrations Concerning Two New*

Sciences. A copy of this work was taken out of Italy and ultimately published at Leyden in 1638; because publication had been arranged without Galileo's knowledge or consent, no punitive measures were taken against him. Totally blind in his final years, but with his mind still vigorous, he died on 8 January 1642, in his seventy-eighth year.

2

The Intellectual Background

We have raised a number of questions concerning the nature and originality of Galileo's contribution to the development of science, and, more generally, about the nature and "revolutionary" character of the scientific revolution, and, finally, about the implications of this case for the understanding of science generally. But in order to deal with these questions —in order to assess fully the similarities and differences, the continuities and discontinuities, between Galileo and his predecessors, to determine what was innovative in his views, and to expose the reasoning underlying those transitions—it is necessary first to survey some of the major relevant ideas of the intellectual tradition forming the background of Galileo's work. These traditional ideas, which we will examine in this chapter, are: the philosophical systems of Plato and Aristotle; certain fourteenth-century views which were developed out of criticisms of Aristotle; and the astronomical theories of Aristotle, Ptolemy, Copernicus, and Tycho Brahe. A further intellectual influence—that of Archimedes—will be discussed in chapter 3.

Summarizing such views raises two kinds of problems. First, the interpretation of specific points—especially in such thinkers as Plato and Aristotle—is often a complex and controversial matter. In a work of the present sort it is impossible to take account of such complexities in all cases. We shall therefore limit ourselves to presenting that interpretation which seems most generally accepted by scholars.

But, second, it is necessary to distinguish between what a certain thinker actually held (that is, the best interpretation scholars can arrive at of what he actually held), and what he was believed to have held by a later thinker. For what a certain historical figure *thinks* an earlier writer believed may, in the light of scholarship, be demonstrably not what that earlier writer really *did* think. For example, we will find Galileo frequently indicating agreement with Plato; and some historians have used such passages as evidence for interpreting Galileo as a "Platonist," and for concluding that the scientific revolution arose out of a Platonic reaction against Aristotelianism. In order to assess such interpretations, we not only will have to compare Galileo's views with those of Plato, but also will have to ask how Galileo himself (and his contemporaries) interpreted Plato's doctrines. That is, we will have to ask whether—even if Galileo and his contemporaries *thought* they were being "Platonists"—we are really entitled to say that they, and the scientific revolution, really *were* Platonic.

Particularly in the cases of Plato and Aristotle, this chapter will focus on more general aspects of the views discussed; in some cases, discussion of specific points, or of contrasts with or implications for subsequent thought, will be postponed until later.

Plato

Plato's views about the nature and structure of the physical universe—or the realm of "Becoming" or "Change," as he called it—are found primarily in his *Timaeus*, presumably a late work. However, those views are presented within the framework of the general theory of "Forms" which, with considerable variations, permeates his other writings. What I will try to do here is to sketch, in five closely related propositions, the core of that general view, leaving some of the more specific details of his view of the realm of Becoming to be discussed where they are relevant.

PROPOSITION 1. *There are absolute standards ("Forms," "Essences," "Ideas," "Universals") which hold for all men and all times, independently of human opinions about them.* This characteristically Platonic doctrine apparently stemmed from the reaction on the part of Plato's master, Socrates, against the relativism of the Sophists, as typified in the statement, attributed to Protagoras, that "man is the measure of all things, of things that are that they are, and of things that are not that they are not." That is, each man can construct or invent his own set of ideas; those ideas may or may not agree with the views of other men, but, apart from such factors as emotional preference or rhetorical persuasion, there are no objective grounds for choosing one set of ideas over any other. For Plato, on the contrary, there is a set of ideas which, whether or not anyone accepts or is even aware of them, are absolutely true. They are to be discovered, not merely invented or constructed.

PROPOSITION 2. *These Forms exist not only as ideas which are in or obtained by the mind, but also in a realm independent of this spatio-temporal world.* When the Platonic Forms are spoken of as "Ideas," we must not suppose that they are merely contents of minds (which we will indicate by speaking of "ideas," uncapitalized): Forms, truths, are more than mere mental contents, in the sense that a proposition or Idea would be true even if there were no minds to know them.[1] Indeed, for Plato, an Idea (or proposition) would be true even if there were no *things* exemplifying them: "$2+2=4$" would be true even if there were no pairs of pairs of things in existence. In short, *even if there were neither things nor minds, the Forms would still exist.* This is simply another aspect of the doctrine, noted already in proposition 1, that mind discovers truths (Forms); it does not construct or invent them.

PROPOSITION 3. *The world of spatio-temporal entities is the realm of change, of flow, of "Becoming"; of it we can have only belief or opinion, not knowledge. Knowledge is of the unchanging—that is, of the Forms, the realm of "Being."* Truths—Forms and their relations—are eternal; and that means, for Plato, unchanging—not relative to a particular person's opinion, or the fads of an era or a culture. The world of our sensory experience, on the other hand, is a realm of change, of "Becoming," rather than (as is the realm of Forms) of "Being." Everything in it is in a constant state of flux; in order to talk or think about it, however, we must apply fixed concepts to things which, inasmuch as they are in constant change, do not fulfill those concepts perfectly. Knowledge can consist only in grasping Ideas and their relations; and these are fixed, eternal, and never fit precisely the diversity and change of things in the spatio-temporal world of change.

PROPOSITION 4. *Forms are principles of explanation of things, both descriptively and prescriptively.* Forms are principles of description, in the sense that we use them, and must use them (or at least our imperfect mental imitations of them), to characterize, classify, and think about things, even though the things of this world never exemplify them perfectly: for Plato, nothing in this world really deserves the name or description we give it. Indeed, if a thing had no characteristics at all (exemplified no Form at all), not only could we not think about it; it could not even be said to exist. Conversely, for Plato, things in this realm of change can be said to "exist" only *to a degree*—namely, the degree to which they exemplify a Form. This notion of "degrees of existence" is foreign to most modern thought, for which something either exists or does not exist. In Plato's system, the notion of "degrees of existence" acquires technical status in the following way. A spatio-temporal individual exemplifies ("participates in" or "imitates," depending on which of two highly controversial interpretations is accepted) a Form —say the Form of "Man," and to the extent of that (always imperfect) exemplification, is a man. But Forms, too, have (always perfectly exemplified) relations: thus insofar as a spatio-temporal individual exemplifies the Form of Man, he also exemplifies the Form of Animal. Now, all Forms ultimately participate in the Form of Being; hence, to the extent that an individual exemplifies the Form of Man (for example), it also, to that extent, exists, that is, fulfills the Form of Being.

Forms are also prescriptive, in the sense that things in the realm of change are more perfect—morally better—the more completely they fulfill their Form. Thus, to be a good man is to fulfill more completely the Form of Man. (As all other Forms participate in the Form of Being, so that Form in turn participates in a higher Form, the Idea of the Good.

Thus, insofar as something is, it is good.) Forms, then, are not only patterns of description; they also serve as standards of evaluation.

In terms of the cosmology of the *Timaeus*—which Plato may or may not have intended us to take absolutely literally—there were in the beginning (that is, before the creation of the realm of Becoming) two separate realms. On the one hand, there was the realm of Forms—perfect and unchanging patterns or ideals (though, of course, not existing in space and time). On the other hand, there was (to the extent that something entirely characterless can even be said to be) the totally formless "Receptacle."[2] (In the *Timaeus*, the Receptacle is referred to as "Space"; in another dialogue, *Philebus*, the factor corresponding to the Receptacle is referred to as the "Indefinite.") Copies of the Forms could be imposed, to some extent, on the Receptacle—but only to some extent. For the one characteristic—a purely negative one—of the Receptacle was to resist and limit such imposition. This it would do, if the occasion arose, in two ways: first, no form could be imposed on it perfectly; and second, when such imposition did occur, even to the limited extent to which that was possible, the Receptacle would continue to resist and gradually work out of that form, decay from it. (That process of decay from embodied form constitutes Time, a "moving image of eternity.")

Both the Forms and the Receptacle are purely static and passive. However, there is also an active agency in the universe, the "Demiurge," the Platonic equivalent of God. The Demiurge, seeing that the Forms were good, and "Desiring, then, that all things should be good and, so far as might be, nothing imperfect," used the Forms as a blueprint for the imposition of form on the Receptacle, for the creation of the realm of Becoming. He thus brought the Receptacle "from disorder into order, since he judged that order was in every way the better" (*Timaeus*, 30A). But unlike the God of most medieval thinkers, Plato's Demiurge is limited in two important ways: (a) He was responsible neither for the creation of the material of the world, nor for the Plan according to which he designed it; both existed independently of him; and (b) because of the nature of the Receptacle, the Demiurge was unable to create a world (impose forms on the Receptacle) perfectly. The Platonic God was absolutely good, but not also omnipotent; and it was largely for this reason that the medieval philosophers, attempting to reconcile their faith with the dictates of reason, ultimately rejected the Platonic philosophy as incompatible with Christianity.

PROPOSITION 5. *Knowledge of the Forms cannot be obtained from sensory experience, but must in the last analysis be obtained by reason (or, perhaps more accurately, by rational reflection or reminiscence).* Whether intended as myth or as literal doctrine, a view to which Plato frequently appealed was his "Doctrine of Recollection [or Reminiscence]." According to this view, the souls of men—active agencies analogous to, but on a lesser scale than, the Demiurge—were exposed to the Forms before being born into this world. The shock of birth, however, made them forget that exposure, that knowledge, to a large degree. We are vaguely reminded of the Forms in our sensory experience; but a knowledge of them—that is, a memory of them—can be obtained, to at least some extent, by careful reflection or incisive questioning (hence the appropriateness of the dialogue form, with its Socratic cross-examination).

Thus sensory experience can be a first stage in the acquisition of knowledge, awakening us as it can to reflection. But it itself cannot provide us with this knowledge. Not only are the Forms not realized perfectly in this world, so that we could not discover them through sensory experience of that world; we also could not get knowledge of them through sense experience because talking or thinking about the things in our experience *presupposes* a knowledge of the Forms. As we saw above, the Forms are principles of description, explanation, and evaluation; they are thus prerequisites of any attempt to describe, explain, or evaluate. Sensory experience, in short, cannot be the source of knowledge of the Forms, of truth, because intelligible sensory experience presupposes such knowledge. (Hence the necessity that they be in our minds, however vaguely we are conscious of them, *prior* to experience.)

These, then, are the major features of Plato's general philosophical outlook which are relevant to the discussion of

Galileo; as was stated above, more specific aspects of Plato's views, particularly of the nature and processes of the realm of change, and of the ways of knowing that realm, will be discussed in the appropriate places.

Aristotle

For our purposes, the views of Aristotle may be considered to rest on three basic distinctions.

1. *Form vs. matter.* Whereas for Plato the individual entity had existence only insofar as it exemplified a form, for Aristotle the individual entity, or *substance,* is what is ultimately real in a primary sense. Any individual thing can be looked upon as "matter" possessing "form" (or forms); but, in contrast with Plato's philosophy, forms never exist except as embodied in matter.[3] The distinction between form and matter is in most contexts a relative one: for the sculptor, the bronze is "matter" to be formed; but from another point of view, it is both form and matter. However, we can distinguish a "prime matter" which, while never found separate from some form or other, is ultimately that which is formed.[4]

2. *Essence vs. accident.* Some forms which individuals possess are more fundamental than others, in the sense that when that individual is classified according to that form, the resulting classification is a more natural one. Thus, for Socrates to be classified as human is a more fundamental way of considering him than to classify him as snub-nosed: the former characteristic has to do with his essence; the latter is only an accident. In his *Categories* Aristotle gives the following list of types of accidents: quantity, quality, relation, place, time, position, state, action, and affection.

This pair of distinctions, form-matter and essence-accident, is fundamental to an understanding of Aristotle's theory of knowledge. What we know initially are individual substances; however, the mind has the power, by observing those individuals, to construct general concepts or universals. In this process of constructing universals, the first requisite is sense-perception; this, however, though necessary for gaining knowledge, is not sufficient; memory is also required, "and out of frequently repeated memories of the same thing develops experience" (*Posterior Analytics*, 100a4), which is "the universal now stabilized in its entirety in the soul" (ibid., 100a6). Thus we pass by a process of "induction" or "abstraction" from particulars to universals, and on to higher and higher universals until we reach the highest of all, the "primary premises" which lie at the foundation of all scientific knowledge, and whose truth and primacy are grasped by "intuition." (There are primary premises which hold for scientific knowledge in general, and also ones which hold only for specific sciences.) Once we have achieved this level, we may work down again by a process of logical demonstration. Scientific knowledge, in particular, is concerned with knowledge of essences rather than of accidents; and essences are related to one another in necessary truths. Thus, science is concerned with necessary, and not merely probable, propositions.

3. *Potentiality vs. actuality.* This distinction can best be explained in terms of three uses to which Aristotle puts it.

a. Prime matter is pure potentiality; that is, it is capable of receiving any form. Individual substances, however, are limited in their capacities to receive forms: thus an unmusical man may become musical, but a rock cannot.

b. In book 3 of his *Physics*, Aristotle gives an analysis of the concept of infinity. There is no such thing, he holds, as an actual infinite: for example, no body is actually infinite in size; no body consists of an actually infinite number of parts. On the contrary, when something is said to be infinite, what is meant is that there is a process which can always be carried further. "The infinite turns out to be the contrary of what it is said to be. It is not what has nothing outside it that is infinite, but what always has something outside it. . . . Our definition then is as follows: A quantity is infinite if it is such that we can always take a part outside what has been already taken" (*Physics*, 206b34–207a8). That is, infinity has to do not with any *actuality*, but with a *potentiality* of always going further. This analysis provides a main basis of his arguments against Zeno's Paradoxes: they rest on the assumptions that space—more particularly, a spatial line—consists of an actual infinity of points, and that time con-

sists of an actual infinity of moments. Aristotle holds that
these assumptions are mistaken: to speak of an infinity of
points in a continuum is merely to say that there is always
a potentiality of further subdividing the continuum, not that
it consists of an actual infinity of elements. We will see other
applications of this analysis of infinity later.

c. But the most striking use to which Aristotle puts his
distinction between potentiality and actuality is found in his
analysis of motion or change. In any case of change, Aristotle maintains, there must be two "contraries": the form of
the substance at the beginning of the change (which the
medievals called the *terminus a quo*, the "terminus from
which"), and the contrary form at the end (the *"terminus ad
quem"*). But in addition to these factors, which have to do
with the alteration that takes place in change, there must
also be a factor accounting for the continuity underlying
that alteration; this factor is called the *substratum* of the
change. Thus, in the change of color of a leaf in autumn, the
leaf is the substratum of the change, and the contraries are
green and yellow. Now the substance at the beginning of the
change—the substratum and the initial form, or *terminus a
quo*—can be looked upon as being in a state of *privation* of,
or relative to, the terminal form, though as having the
potentiality of fulfilling it. Thus Aristotle arrives at a general
definition of motion or change as "the actualization of the
potential, insofar as it is potential" (*Physics*, 201a10–11), the
last clause calling attention to the fact that substances are
limited in their potentialities. (It is important to emphasize
that there are definite initial and terminal forms in change,
and that those forms are spoken of as "contrary" to one
another.)

Aristotle distinguishes two general kinds of change or
motion. On the one hand, there is coming-to-be and passing-
away, or generation and corruption; this kind of change may
be called *substantial*. Even here, however, as in all change,
there must be a substratum, which is ultimately prime matter. The other kind of change is *accidental*; of this, there are
three subtypes: alteration or qualitative change; increase or
decrease, or quantitative change; and locomotion, or change
of place (to which our modern word "motion" is generally

restricted). Our interest will ultimately be on the last of these, which Aristotle himself claims is the fundamental type. His general analysis, however, applies to all four.

As in all science, according to Aristotle, an understanding of motion requires an understanding of its causes. Here it is necessary to refer to Aristotle's distinction of four kinds of causes, or senses in which the word "cause" may be used, or in which one can ask for a causal explanation: (a) the *material* cause (for example, the bronze which will be formed by the sculptor is the material cause of the statue); (b) the *formal* cause (the statue's shape, and, more generally, the form of a thing); (c) the *efficient* cause (the hands and tools of the sculptor); and (d) the *final* cause (the plan or purpose of the sculptor). For Aristotle, all four of these questions must be asked in regard to any case of any of the four types of change (as long as the event is a natural one): there are final causes, purposes, for example, even in physical nature. Any case of any kind of motion will, furthermore, be either violent or natural. That is, bodies will, under certain circumstances, move only if pushed or pulled by something else; under other circumstances, they may move "by their own nature." In order to understand this view of motion, we must first analyze Aristotle's ideas of "nature," "natural motion," and the circumstances under which the latter will take place.

"Nature," according to Aristotle, "is a source or cause of being moved and of being at rest in that to which it belongs primarily, in virtue of itself and not in virtue of a concomitant attribute" (*Physics*, 192b21–23). Thus nature is a principle of movement in any thing, by virtue of which that thing alters, grows, or changes place; and that principle must, furthermore, be intrinsic in the sense that it is not an accidental accompaniment (even an internal one) of the thing. (This sense of the word—which we still find in such expressions as "human nature" and "the nature of the beast"— must be distinguished from another common modern sense, in which it refers to the physical universe as a whole, as in such expressions as "physical nature" or "the laws of nature.") Aristotle identifies nature with form, and more particularly with the essential form of a thing. Thus form

tends in Aristotle to be more than merely a passive factor
as it was for Plato; rather, it is an active agency, a power of
movement; it becomes analogous to what Plato called "soul."
And indeed, for higher types of beings—plants, animals, and
men—the (essential) form is called, respectively, the "vege-
tative soul," the "animal [or sensitive] soul," and the "rational soul." Form (and therefore nature) is further associated in Aristotle with the function of things—the role they
play in a larger whole—and thus with purpose. Hence "nature" takes on aspects of final as well as formal and efficient
causation. Thus the essential form of the eye is intimately
related to its function of seeing; and the fulfillment of that
form (potentiality) contributes to the fulfillment of the
larger organism of which the eye is a part, just as the fulfillment, by the parts of the eye, of their individual forms
or functions contributes to the functioning of the eye as
a whole.

In the light of this, it is easy to see why, when the Christian thinkers of the thirteenth century tried to reconcile
their faith with the dictates of reason, it was Aristotle's
philosophy which seemed most appealing as a rational base.
For, in terms of his view, it was possible to interpret the
universe as having a plan or purpose—God's plan—and
everything in it as contributing its part to the fulfillment of
that plan. Man, in particular, could do his part, fulfill his
natural potentiality, or not; to do so was morally good, not
to do so was the reverse. But Aristotle's philosophy was
amenable to a Christian (or, for that matter, a Jewish or
Mohammedan) interpretation not only in this general aspect,
but also in a multitude of details. Indeed, although there
was room for many disagreements with Aristotle on detailed topics, and still more for disagreements as to interpretations of his words, the thirteenth-century Christian philosophers could accept his general system wholeheartedly except for two major points. First, Aristotle held the universe
to be eternal, rather than having been created from nothing
by God (for, Aristotle maintained, something cannot be
created from nothing). And second, Aristotle's "Prime Mover"
—the being which, while immovable himself, was ultimately

responsible for the existence of motion in the universe—was not a personal God, interested in the moral fates of individual men and occasionally interfering with events in the universe. On the contrary, he was eternally involved, in his immovable way, with thinking about thinking. But these two objectionable tenets could, the medievals held, be rejected without damage to the rest of the Aristotelian system; and they combined that remnant—or, more accurately, each thinker combined his interpretation of that system— with Christian belief (or his own interpretation thereof) into impressively coherent syntheses. Variations of interpretation of Aristotle and of Christian doctrine, of course, led to vigorous controversy; and by the fourteenth century, as we shall see, alternatives to some of the most fundamental aspects of Aristotelian thought were being actively considered. Such controversy took place in a fairly liberal atmosphere, with little or no threat of persecution; but it is easy to understand how the day might have come when criticisms of the foundations of Aristotle's system might appear dangerous to the foundations of Christian faith itself.

To return now to Aristotle himself, our next step in developing his view of motion is to examine his concept of "place." The place of a thing, Aristotle says, is defined by the inner boundary of the container of that thing—as long as that containing thing itself is not in motion; for then the place of the thing would be ambiguous. Thus the place of a piece of wood floating in a running stream must be referred, not to the immediately containing water, but to the stationary bank. In short, "place" is defined as "the innermost motionless boundary of that which contains" (*Physics*, 212a20).

In the light of these ideas of "nature" and "place," let us outline the structure of the universe as Aristotle conceived it, and the natural motions of the things contained therein. The universe is finite in size (it could not be infinite; for nothing is actually infinite) and spherical in shape (for reasons which we shall examine later). Beyond the outer limit of its outer boundary, there is nothing, not even a void; for, since place is referred to a containing body and there is no container of the universe, the universe is not in any place. At the center of the universe is the earth; the periphery is bounded by the sphere (or rather, outermost layer of the single universal sphere) of the fixed stars. Immediately within that sphere (and with no vacant space between) is the sphere (or, more accurately, as we shall see later, the system of spheres) containing the planet Saturn; next in descending order toward the center are the spheres of Jupiter, Mars, the sun, Venus, Mercury, and the moon—all concentric around the center of the universe, which, for reasons that will become apparent shortly, coincides with the center of the earth. These heavenly spheres rotate, each with its own uniform speed, around the center forever. That rotation "in place" is the only kind of change undergone in the Heavens, which are thus "incorruptible"; everything there is composed of a single element, ether, so that there cannot be a coming-together and separation of elements.

Beneath the inner boundary of the lunar sphere, however, things are composed of four elements: fire, air, water, and earth (which, in their elemental forms, are purer than the things we ordinarily call by those names). Each of these elements has its "natural place": fire in the spherical layer just beneath the lunar sphere, air in the next layer, water in the next, and earth, being heavy, at the center. This is why the center of the earth coincides with the center of the universe—because that is the natural place of earthy things.

If the elements in this sublunar realm were left to follow their own natures, they would become and remain stratified in the layers which constitute their natural places, where they would remain at rest. However, they are kept stirred up, largely by the motion of the lunar sphere, and ultimately by the motion of the outermost sphere; and so they become removed from their natural places and mixed with each other into the things we know. Nevertheless, the natural tendency of an element is always to return to its natural place, the *terminus ad quem* of its change of place, and there come to rest. (If a body is composed of several elements, it will of course tend to move to the natural place of its predominant element.) Thus fire, being by nature light, moves up to the "center [really spherical layer] of levity" or lightness; earth moves down to the "center of gravity" or heaviness; and air and water move in appropriate directions toward their natural places, depending on where they begin that natural motion. "How can we account for the motion of light things and heavy things to their proper situations? The reason for it is that they have a natural tendency respectively towards a certain position: and this constitutes the essence of lightness and heaviness, the former being determined by an upward, the latter by a downward, tendency" (*Physics*, 255b13–17). And so, as the natural motion of ether is "around the center," and, being circular, is perpetual, the sublunar elements have natural motions "toward the center" or "away from the center," and those motions have definite beginning and end points. (Thus the universe is spherical, partly because that shape is simple and "perfect" and "most appropriate to its substance and also by nature primary" [*On the Heavens*, 286b10–12], partly because that figure can undergo the minimal type of change, rotation "in place," and partly in order to mark out unambiguously a central point to which the element earth may be directed by its nature.)

In terms of later thought, it is interesting to note that gravity, for Aristotle, is a relationship between a material body of a certain sort (earthy, that is, heavy) and a spatial location. Thus, for Aristotle, even if there were no earth at the center of the universe, a piece of that element located elsewhere in the sublunar domain would still tend to move toward that center: "If one were to remove the earth to where the moon is now, the various fragments of earth would each move not towards it but to the place in which it now is" (*On the Heavens*, 310b2–5). This view is to be contrasted not only with the Newtonian view, according to which gravity is a relationship between material bodies, of any sort, but also from the view, expressed in Plato's *Timaeus*, that gravity is a relationship between *like* material objects (on the principle that "like attracts like"). For this latter view, for example, earthy matter would be attracted to earthy matter, but not, say, to lunar. We will find this important view being revived by critics of Aristotle in the late middle ages and adopted, in one form or another, by many sixteenth- and seventeenth-century thinkers.

Prime matter conjoined with the fundamental forms "hot" and "dry" is the element fire; with "hot" and "wet," is air; with "cold" and "wet," is water; and with "cold" and "dry," is earth. These fundamental forms constitute the nature of these elements; that is, they determine, in each case, in ways that Aristotle does not always make clear, the properties and behavior of the elements (and bodies composed of them). In particular, they determine whether an element is "heavy" or "light," and therefore the character of its natural motion. The elements can be converted into one another by the replacement in any one of them of one of the members of the contrary pairs cold-hot and wet-dry by the other.

In regard to naturally falling (or rising) bodies, the question arises as to whether, and precisely how, the speed of fall (or rise) depends on the "degree of heaviness" or weight (or, for naturally rising bodies, on the "degree of lightness") of the body. Aristotle makes a number of scattered remarks on this subject, though always in passing, in the context of other arguments. Nevertheless, inasmuch as this problem will be especially important in discussing Galileo, it will be advisable to look at Aristotle's own words on the subject.

> We see the same weight or body moving faster [in fall] than another for two reasons, either because there is a difference in what it moves through, as between water, air, and earth, or because, other things being equal, the moving body differs from the other owing to excess of weight or lightness. (*Physics*, 215a25–28)

That is, the speed is affected, in ways which we will examine shortly, by the medium; but even in the same medium, it is also affected by the weight: of two bodies which are "equal" in all respects except weight, the one with an "excess of weight" or heaviness over the other will move faster (and correspondingly for the rising of light bodies). This effect of weight on speed of fall is further elaborated in the following passage:

bodies which have a greater impulse either of weight or of lightness, if they are alike in other respects, move faster over an equal space, and in the ratio which their magnitudes bear to each other. (*Physics*, 216a12–16)

The implication of this passage is that the speeds of fall are proportional to the weights of the bodies. These same ideas are expressed in *On the Heavens*:

A given weight [in fall] moves a given distance in a given time; a weight which is as great and more moves the same distance in a less time, the times being in inverse proportion to the weights. For instance, if one weight is twice another, it will take half as long over a given movement. (*On the Heavens*, 273b30–274a2)

By absolutely light, then, we mean that which moves upward or to the extremity [i.e., the inner wall of the lunar sphere], and by absolutely heavy that which moves downward or to the center [of the universe]. By lighter or relatively light we mean that one, of two bodies endowed with weight and equal in bulk, which is exceeded by the other in the speed of its downward movement. (*On the Heavens*, 308a29–34)

. . . fire, in whatever quantity, so long as there is no external obstacle, moves upward, and earth downward; and, if the quantity is increased, the movement is the same, though swifter. (*On the Heavens*, 311a20–22)[5]

Thus, bodies in natural motion fall (or rise) toward their natural places with a speed V that is directly proportional to their degree of heaviness H (or lightness) and inversely proportional to the resistance R of the medium; further, the time T of fall (or rise) is inversely proportional to the heaviness (or lightness) of the body. Thus

$$V \propto H/R; \text{ and } T \propto 1/H. \tag{1}$$

It must be remembered that Aristotle does not express his conclusions in such mathematical notation, and that some interpretation of his words is introduced in doing so.

Aristotle is aware that a naturally falling body accelerates (and he holds that rising, light bodies do so also): "earth

moves more quickly the nearer it is to the center, and fire
the nearer it is to the upper place" (*On the Heavens*, 277a28–
30). But according to the quantitative rule just given, we
would expect the speed to remain constant: for the heaviness of the body does not change; and as to the resistance of
the medium, it might even have the effect of *de*celerating
the body. Apart from that rule, we get no clear idea of a
formula for the rate of change of speed. Thus, from the
quotation just given, we do not know whether the body
accelerates at a uniform rate. Furthermore, although that
quotation suggests that the speed achieved through acceleration depends on the distance *left to travel* before arriving at
the natural place, the immediately following sentence gives
the impression that the speed acquired depends on the distance *travelled*: "If movement were [through an] infinite
[distance] speed would be infinite also" (*On the Heavens*,
277a30–31). These questions were debated among his followers and critics, especially in the fourteenth and succeeding centuries—though those writers too, like their master,
seem not to have been clear as to whether there is really
any conflict between relating the speed achieved to distance
fallen, distance left to fall, time fallen, or time left to fall.

The question also arises as to whether the speed of fall (to
say nothing of the rate of change of speed) depends on the
kind of body: is "heaviness" to be interpreted as "weight"
or "density"? If the former, then two bodies of lead, unequal in weight, would fall at unequal speeds, while two
bodies equal in weight, one of lead and the other of wood,
would fall at equal speeds. If, on the other hand, "density"
is what is meant, the exact reverse would be the case: two
bodies of lead, whatever their weights, would fall at the
same speed, while a body of lead and one of wood, even if
equal in weight, would fall at different speeds. Aristotle
seems generally to have been interpreted as holding that the
speed of fall depends on the weight; and there is abundant
textual evidence favoring this interpretation. However, one
is still left with an uneasy feeling as to whether differences
of density, as determined, perhaps, by differences of relative
proportion of elements composing the bodies, might also
have an effect.

Further questions regarding Aristotle's view of natural motion also arise. Suppose a hole were drilled through the earth, passing through its center: if a piece of earth were then dropped through that hole, would it stop abruptly when it reached the center, or would it fly past, decelerate, and then oscillate back and forth about the center with gradually diminishing amplitude and speed until finally coming to a stop at the center? This and other such questions about natural motion were, like those noted above, matters of debate among the followers and critics of Aristotle, especially in the three centuries preceding Galileo.

All motion other than natural requires an extrinsic pushing (or pulling) agent: "Everything that is in motion must be moved by something. For if it has not the source of its motion in itself it is evident that it is moved by something other than itself, for there must be something else that moves it" (*Physics* 241b24–27). Such non-natural motion is termed *violent*. In referring to the pushing agent or motive force as "extrinsic," it will be remembered, we do not mean to imply that it must necessarily be outside the body; it can be inside it as long as it is not part of the essential form of the moved body—that is, as long as it does not belong to it "primarily."[6] The greater this force, the faster the body will move: "if a given force move a given weight a certain distance in a certain time and half the distance in half the time, half the motive power will move half the weight the same distance in the same time" (*Physics*, 250a4–7). But such agents must always be in contact with the thing moved: for Aristotle, one thing cannot exert causal influence—at least in the sense of efficient causation—on another without touching it; there is no such thing as action at a distance.

In the case of both natural and violent motion, the medium resists the motion of the body: "The medium causes a difference [in the speed] of the body because it impedes the moving thing, most of all if it is moving in the opposite direction, but in a secondary degree even if it is at rest; and especially a medium that is not easily divided, i.e., a medium that is somewhat dense" (*Physics*, 215a28–32). This suggests, at least, that the denser the medium, the greater the resistance.

Taking these considerations together, it appears that the speed V of a violently moved body is directly proportional to the pushing force F and inversely proportional to the resistance R of the medium:

$$V \propto F/R,$$

or, introducing a constant of proportionality k,

$$V = k(F/R).$$

In such cases, by appropriately choosing our units of measurement of F and R, we can make $k = 1$, so that

$$V = F/R. \tag{2}$$

This simple form of the relationship is in fact the interpretation of Aristotle given by many of his fourteenth century commentators and critics, as we shall see below. Nevertheless, it again imposes some doubtful interpretation on his view: for example, the formula holds only if F is greater than R; and perhaps Aristotle might have said that F must be enough greater than R to set the body in motion in the first place.

Comparing equations (1) and (2), we see that the cases of natural and violent motion are parallel, the cause of motion in the former being the natural heaviness H (or lightness) of the body, while in the latter the cause is an extrinsic motive force F.

We will postpone discussion of problems regarding Aristotle's conception of violent motion until the next section. For Galileo and some other sixteenth and seventeenth century writers for whom all bodies are characterized by heaviness—lightness being, according to them, not a positive property, but merely a lesser degree of heaviness—the problems clustering around natural motion become the *problem of falling bodies.* And we shall find that the problems in Aristotle's treatment of violent motion will, for the sixteenth and seventeenth centuries, be rechristened the *problem(s) of projectile motion.*

With the imposition of a certain minimal amount of plausible interpretation, all the preceding discussion of motion, celestial and sublunar, natural and violent, may be summarized in the following *Aristotelian Laws of Motion.*

Law 1. *Every sublunar body not in its natural place will move by its own nature along a radius of the universe to its natural place (or the natural place of its predominant element) and there come to rest, unless impeded by a contrary agency. The fall (or rise) will take place according to the relationship*

$$V = H/R, \text{ and } T = 1/H,$$

where V is the speed of fall or rise, H the degree of heaviness or lightness, R the resistance of the medium, and T the time of fall or rise. *These relationships, however, must be supplemented by an unspecified term having to do with the acceleration of the falling or rising body.*

Law 2. *A sublunar body will move violently if and only if it is acted upon by an extrinsic contact force (which is large enough to start the body moving in the first place), according to the relationship*

$$V = F/R,$$

where F is the motive force.

Law 3. *Heavenly bodies move naturally in uniform circular motion around the center of the universe.*

These laws are to be contrasted with the modern principle of inertia in the following respects.

a. For Aristotle, different kinds of substance (different elements) have different kinds of natural motion: earth toward the center; fire away from the center and to the upper reaches of the sublunar domain; the intermediate elements up or down to their natural places, depending on the place of origin of their movement; and ether around the center. According to the principle of inertia, *all* bodies, of whatever composition, will remain at rest or continue in uniform rectilinear motion unless acted on by an extrinsic force.

b. For the Aristotelian first law, the only kind of natural rectilinear motion is the up or down motion (along a radius of the universe) of the elements. For the principle of inertia, "natural" motion—in the sense of motion which continues without an extrinsic pushing force—can be in any direction. Thus the Aristotelian view is intimately tied in with the view of the universe as finite, so that particular locations (e.g., a center) and directions (e.g., up and down) are definitely marked out. The principle of inertia is compatible with, though it does not require, an infinite universe in which no points or directions are singled out as special in any way.[7]

c. The natural rectilinear motion of the first Aristotelian law is accelerated; that of the principle of inertia is uniform.

d. For Aristotle, rectilinear motion, being a case of natural change, must have a *terminus a quo* and a *terminus ad quem*: "there cannot be a continuous rectilinear motion that is eternal" (*Physics*, 263a3). For the principle of inertia, a body moving and free of extrinsic forces will continue in uniform rectilinear motion forever.

e. For Aristotle, "violent" motion will continue only so long as there is a contact pushing force acting on the body; when that force is removed, the body will come to rest. (However, we will find in the next section that there are problems with this view.) That is, $F \propto V$. For the principle of inertia, forces are not necessary to *keep* the body in motion, but only to *change* its motion (either to speed it up or slow it down or change its direction); that is, force is proportional to change of velocity (including now not only speed but also direction), that is, acceleration: $F \propto a$.

f. It follows from (*e*) that for Aristotle the ultimate natural state of a sublunar body (though not of a heavenly one) is a state of rest: even natural motions always end in that state, and occur only after a body has been violently moved from its natural place. For the principle of inertia, rest *and* a certain kind of motion (namely, uniform rectilinear) are equally "natural" in the sense of not requiring an extrinsic force for their continuation.

There are some further points in Aristotle's system that are important for our purposes.

(*i*) On the basis of a number of arguments, he contends that there cannot be any empty place, that is, void: the universe is full. One such argument is the following: a void would be a region in which there is no medium; if there were any such region, then the resistance R to a body moving through it would be zero, and the equation $V = F/R$, with $R = 0$, implies that V would be infinite; but an actual infinite is impossible, and therefore there cannot be a void. This argument should illustrate the close knit of concepts in the Aristotelian system ("void," "infinite," laws of motion).

(*ii*) No unnatural process can continue forever, but must come to an eventual stop: "clearly nothing which . . . is unnatural ever continues for an infinity of time" (*On the Heavens*, 288b24–25). This principle underlies the proposition that violent motion must come to a stop. As to the converse proposition—that whatever is natural is everlasting—this holds only for special types of motions in which there are no definite beginning or terminal points, no contraries, as in circular motion. Natural changes in which there is a definite beginning and terminal point will not be eternal.

(*iii*) A simple body can have only one natural motion: "naturally a thing moves in one way, while its unnatural movements are manifold" (*On the Heavens*, 300a26–27).

(*iv*) When a body has two competing tendencies to motion, one will predominate completely over the other. For example, if a body is thrown horizontally from a tower, its path will not be a composite or resultant of a horizontal "violent" component and a "natural" one of gravity; the horizontal motion will occur first, and then, when it can no longer continue, the downward tendency will take over. It is not clear how strongly Aristotle adhered to this proposition, since in specific discussions he often in effect denies it. However, it does seem to have been accepted by many of his medieval followers, at least in principle, and plays an important part in many of the debates which we will be discussing.

It is important to recognize the extent to which Aristotle's conclusions seemed, consistently with his general view of the method of gaining knowledge, to come from observation. "We see with our eyes . . . that earthy things sink to the bottom of all things and move towards the center" (*On the*

Heavens, 311b20–21). We know from experience that, except for the case of rising and falling, things will not move unless they are pushed, and that we must keep on pushing them or they will quickly come to a halt. Simplicio faithfully represents the position of his master when he asks

> who is there so blind as not to see that earthy and watery parts, as heavy things, move naturally downward—that is to say toward the center of the universe, assigned by nature itself as the end and terminus of straight motion downward? Who does not likewise see fire and air move directly upward toward the arc of the moon's orbit, as the natural end of motion upward? (*Two Chief World Systems*, pp. 32–33)

(On the other hand, should we not ask, correspondingly, Who has followed by observation the motion of a body free from all external forces, and found that it continues forever in a straight line? What, then, is the relation of the principle of inertia to experience or observation? Or is there any? It is at this point, particularly, that doubts begin to arise regarding Mach's interpretation of the scientific revolution as an empiricist reaction against philosophical rationalism.) Certainly in some cases Aristotle seems to draw more from observation than, to our eyes, is clearly forthcoming from it. Thus he claims that "it is a matter of observation that a natural body possesses a principle of movement" (*On the Heavens*, 304b14); but what we see is that it moves, and we do not observe its "principle" of movement. Again, he claims that "our eyes tell us that the heavens revolve in a circle" (*On the Heavens*, 271b5); but what we see is that the stars rise in the east and set in the west: is this because the heavens revolve around the stationary earth from east to west, or because the earth revolves under a stationary sky from west to east? We will find Aristotle eliminating the second alternative; but that elimination is necessary, above and beyond what we see, in order to guarantee the truth of the first. Even the claim that "earthy things . . . move towards the center" will eventually prove to involve profound assumptions, particularly about gravity and the finitude of the universe, that go beyond observation—or at least beyond the most immediate observation.

Developments in the Middle Ages

With regard to the development of early modern science, the most important difficulties of Aristotle's system are those having to do with his treatment of violent motion. According to his analysis, violent motion requires the continuous application of a contact motive force; the question therefore obviously arises as to why bodies do in fact continue to move "violently" after being released by the propelling agent. Aristotle himself raises the problem:

> If everything that is in motion with the exception of things that move themselves is moved by something else, how is it that some things, e.g. things thrown, continue to be in motion when their movent is no longer in contact with them? (*Physics*, 266b27–30)

Why does a thrown object not immediately assume its natural motion and fall to the ground once released by the throwing hand? For at that moment the pushing force responsible for the violent motion is removed, and only the natural tendency of the object remains. Aristotle mentions three possible answers to this objection to his theory.

1. "That the movent in such cases moves something else at the same time, that the thrower, e.g. also moves the air, and that this in being moved is also a movent" (*Physics*, 266b30–32). The hand moves the air in front of it as well as the stone, and the air in turn, allegedly, continues to carry the stone along as though in a stream. However, Aristotle raises a fatal objection against this proposal: "it would be no more possible for this second thing [e.g., the air] than for the original thing [the stone] to be in motion when the original movent [the hand] is not in contact with it or moving it: all the things moved would have to be in motion simultaneously and also to have ceased simultaneously to be in motion when the original movent ceases to move them" (*Physics*, 266b33–267a1). That is, the air, too, no less than the stone, would have to cease moving when the pushing

hand stopped; hence the continuation of motion cannot be explained by this theory.

2. Notice that what Aristotle has *not* objected to about this first theory is the possibility that, if the air could continue moving after the hand has stopped pushing it, it could carry the object along. *That* would be all right with him, and so the only problem is to *supplement* the first theory so as to enable the air to continue to move (and, of course, to have its motion die down gradually, so that the stone being carried along by it would not be carried along forever). This supplementation is accomplished by the second view he discusses, and which he himself accepts:

> while we must accept this [first] explanation to the extent of saying that the original movent gives the power of being a movent either to air or to water or to something else of the kind, naturally adapted for imparting and undergoing motion, we must say further that this thing does not cease simultaneously to impart motion and to undergo motion: it ceases to be in motion at the moment when its movent ceases to move it, but it still remains a movent, and so it causes something else consecutive with it to be in motion, and of this again the same may be said. The motion begins to cease when the motive force produced in one member of the consecutive series is at each stage less than that possessed by the preceding member, and it finally ceases when one member no longer causes the next member to be a movent but only causes it to be in motion. . . . motion of this kind takes place in air and water. (*Physics*, 267a2–16)

That is, the air or water moved, along with the projectile, by the original mover receives, because of its special nature, the power to act as a mover; this power, communicated successively in decreasing amounts to the air beyond, continues to carry the projectile along by contact action until the transmitted power is exhausted.

3. Aristotle also mentions another view: "Some say that [the source of continued motion] is 'mutual replacement'" (*Physics*, 267a16), a view presented in Plato's *Timaeus* (79A–80C; *cf.*, Cornford, *Plato's Cosmology*, pp. 315–27), and

which, interestingly, may have its roots in Sicilian medical doctrines (Cornford, pp. 307–27). Generally known as the "antiperistasis theory," this view holds that a "mutual replacement" occurs between the projectile and the air: the thrown object pushes air out from in front of it as it moves; that air displaces other air; and, since nature abhors a vacuum, air rushes into the place that otherwise would be evacuated by the forward-moving object, and thus propels the object along as a contact pushing force. Aristotle seems to believe that such a process might occur and—just as with view (1)—might have an effect in keeping the body moving *if* the theory is supplemented by his own view (2):

> the difficulty raised cannot be solved otherwise than in the way we have described [i.e., (2)]. So far as they are affected by "mutual replacement," all the members of the series are moved and impart motion simultaneously. (*Physics*, 267a17–19)[8]

Thus, Aristotle's view seems to be the following: the process described in (1), and perhaps also that described in (3), occur, when—but only when—supplemented by (2), they can account for the fact that a body continues to move even after the original mover is no longer in contact with it. Air and water have a special capacity not only to be moved, but also to receive and transmit, through successive instants, a "power of being a movent." By transmission of that power, the air or water either carries the body along as in a current, or else pushes it along by the antiperistasis mechanism. The power growing successively weaker in each transmission, the object gradually slows down and comes to a stop. But the main point is that the violation of the "no contact force, no motion" principle is only apparent: the air (or water) now plays the role of the contact pushing agent.

It is paradoxical that Aristotle should thus attribute to air the function of maintaining projectile motion; for, as we saw in the preceding section, he also says that it resists motion. Air thus plays two contradictory roles. This and other considerations led the sixth-century Byzantine philosopher, John Philoponus, to reject Aristotle's analysis and replace it with a view according to which "some incorporeal motive force is imparted by the projector to the projectile, and . . . the air set in motion contributes either nothing at all or else very little to this motion of the projectile" (M. Cohen and I. E. Drabkin, eds., *A Source Book in Greek Science*, p. 223). This view appears again in the Latin West in the first half of the fourteenth century, where it acquired a wide influence through the writings of John Buridan, rector of the University of Paris. Buridan, like Philoponus before him, rejects both the air-current and antiperistasis views, even when supplemented by Aristotle's "power of being a movent" view. In addition to objecting against the contradiction of having the air act both as mover and resistance, Buridan appeals to "many experiences" to refute the role of air in the continuance of projectile motion. Against the antiperistasis view, he argues that a spinning top or a wheel rotating in place continue to move long after the pushing hand that set them rotating has been removed; but in such cases, there is no room for air to rush in behind. A spear pointed at both ends should not travel as far when thrown as one with a blunt back end, because "the air would be easily divided by the sharpness" (M. Clagett, ed., *The Science of Mechanics in the Middle Ages*, p. 533) and so could not push efficiently. A sailor standing on the deck of a fast-moving ship feels the resistance of the air from the direction in which the ship is moving, but does not feel the push of air from behind, as the antiperistasis theory requires. And as to the air-current theory, it cannot account for the case of the rotating wheel either. It fails to account for the continued movement of a ship, for

> if [the ship] were covered by a cloth and the cloth with the ambient air were withdrawn, the ship would not stop its motion on this account. And even if the ship were loaded with grain or straw and were moved by the ambient air, then that air ought to blow exterior stalks toward the front. But the contrary is evident, for the stalks are blown rather to the rear because of the resisting ambient air. (Clagett, p. 534)

He finds it difficult to believe that easily divided air could sustain the motion of a thousand-pound stone; and finally, the theory seems to require that lighter bodies, like feathers, can be thrown farther than heavier ones. "Experience shows this to be false" (Clagett, p. 534).

In the light of these objections, Buridan, like Philoponus long before, proposes that it is not the air that is responsible for the continuance of projectile motion, but rather what he calls an "impetus" that is communicated to the body by the original mover:

> It seems to me that it ought to be said that the motor in moving a moving body impresses in it a certain impetus or a certain motive force of the moving body [which impetus acts] in the direction toward which the mover was moving the moving body, either up or down, or laterally, or circularly. . . . It is by that impetus that the stone is moved after the projector ceases to move. (Clagett, pp. 534–35)

It is important to notice that, for Buridan, the impetus may be such as to direct the body along a rectilinear or along a circular path.

Although Buridan is not always explicit about, or perhaps even aware of, the extent of his agreement with Aristotle, it is clear that he accepts the latter's view that a power or force must be imparted by the projector if continued violent motion is to be possible: for Buridan, too, there is no motion without a constantly applied force. Where Aristotle went wrong, in Buridan's opinion, was in thinking that that power is communicated to the adjacent air (or water). For even with that power, the two proposed mechanisms by which the air (or water) could in turn move the projectile are inadequate, both to reason and to experience. Rather, the power is communicated directly to the projectile, on which it acts as an invisible, internal (but, in the sense discussed earlier, not intrinsic) motive force. (Technically, this "power" was conceived as being a form, and, more specifically, for Buridan at least, a quality. On these points, however, there was considerable debate among the adherents of the impetus theory.) Aristotle was also correct, in Buridan's eyes, in saying that the power must persist after losing contact with the original mover, and, further, in saying that it must gradually dissipate. But he was vague as to what causes it to dissipate: he merely says that it is reduced at each step in a series of transmissions. Buridan, however, declares that impetus is reduced only in combatting contrary or resisting forces:

> that impetus is continually decreased by the resisting air and by the gravity of the stone, which inclines it in a direction contrary to that in which the impetus was naturally predisposed to move it. Thus the movement of the stone continually becomes slower, and finally that impetus is so diminished or corrupted that the gravity of the stone wins out over it and moves the stone down to its natural place. . . .

> . . . And it also is probable that just as that quality [the impetus] is impressed in the moving body along with the motion by the motor; so with the motion it is remitted, corrupted, or impeded by resistance or a contrary inclination. (Clagett, pp. 535, 537)

Were it not for such corrupting factors, the impetus would remain constant in quantity: "the impetus would last indefinitely if it were not diminished by a contrary resistance or by an inclination to a contrary motion" (Clagett, p. 524). Presumably also, if there were no such factors—if the body were moving in a void, and somehow free of the tendency to move to a natural place—then not only the impetus, but also its effect, the motion, would continue, at a uniform speed, forever, in the direction determined by the impetus. Thus, if it were a rectilinear rather than a circular impetus, such a body would continue in uniform rectilinear motion forever under the influence of the constant impetus.

It is no wonder, then, that immediately upon unearthing the Impetus Theory, Pierre Duhem called attention to the striking parallels between the concept of impetus and that of inertia. Since Buridan's impetus would be preserved except for the degenerative effects of counteragencies, only three main steps appeared necessary to arrive at the principle of inertia, and therefore at a new physics: first, the conception of the possibility of motion in a void or vacuum; second, the abandonment of the idea that there is circular impetus as well as rectilinear; and finally, the abandonment of the idea of impetus as an internal force distinct from the body and maintaining it at constant speed. With those alterations, the Impetus Theory could be seen as transformed into the principle of inertia. Uniform rectilinear motion would be transformed from a violent motion, requiring an extrinsic cause, into a natural one, in the sense that it continues forever without an extrinsic cause, simply by the nature of matter. And the shift from Aristotelian to inertial physics could be seen as a transition from the view that force is the cause of uniform rectilinear *motion* (i.e., of speed or velocity) to the modern view that force is the cause of *change of motion* (i.e., acceleration). If this is a true historical picture, the Impetus Theory would thus stand as a transitional phase between these two traditions: still in the tradition of Aristotelian physics in its view that impetus is an extrinsic cause of motion, but heading toward the modern view in making it an internal and incorporeal force rather than an external, corporeal one.

Further similarities can be found between impetus and the modern concept of momentum. For Buridan also suggests, though without great precision, a quantitative measure of impetus. On the one hand, it appears to be proportional to the speed of the body (as we would expect from someone who, however critical, remains basically within the Aristotelian tradition): "by the amount the motor moves that moving body more swiftly, by the same amount it will impress in it a stronger impetus" (Clagett, p. 535). Further, the greater the quantity of matter in the projectile, the more impetus it can receive: "by the amount more there is of matter, by that amount can the body receive more of that impetus and more intensely" (Clagett, p. 535). These remarks have been interpreted as meaning that the impetus is proportional to the product of the speed and the quantity of matter—which would make impetus a primitive analogue of the modern momentum, the product of velocity and mass. However, this interpretation is at least questionable: for Buridan says only that the quantity of matter determines how much impetus *can* be imparted to the body, not that it determines how much *is* imparted (which presumably can be any amount up to the maximum possible as determined

by the quantity of matter). Just as iron *can* receive more
heat than an equal volume of wood, but need not, so also it
can receive more impetus, but need not, since the amount
conveyed to it may be less than the maximum amount it
could acquire.[9]

Whatever is the case with momentum, the relationships
between impetus and inertia remain; and these are so remarkable that one can hardly help asking the following
questions. If the Impetus Theorists were in this respect so
close to modern physics (and we shall find many more detailed respects in which they were very close indeed), then
why did the transition—if it did, as a matter of historical
fact, take place *via* the three steps mentioned—take so long?
And if it did not take place in this way, why didn't it? In
our approach to these questions, it will prove instructive to
examine some of the obstacles in the way of achieving the
alleged transition. We will then be in a better position to
appraise the Duhemian claim that the Impetus Theory actually was the source of modern physics.

Let us begin by examining in turn each of the three steps
that would have had to be taken.

1. *The conception of the possibility of motion in a void,
that is, of the possibility of motion free of all external forces.*
The Impetus Theorists did speak in terms of such a possibility, which was to some extent opened by their argument
that the medium is unnecessary for the continuation of violent motion. However, in order for the possibility to be fully
open, some alternative to the Aristotelian equation, $V = F/R$,
had to be available and accepted; for otherwise the consequence remained that velocity in a void would be infinite.
We will shortly find that such alternative equations were
being proposed during the Middle Ages; and we will find
Galileo, at the beginning of his investigations, adopting one
of them.

2. *The abandonment of the idea that there is circular
impetus as well as rectilinear.* This step was actually taken
by Giambattista Benedetti, an immediate predecessor of
Galileo. However, for most thinkers, including, as we shall
see, Galileo himself, it was an especially difficult one to take.
In general, circular motion had played a fundamental role

in Greek and medieval science, whereas rectilinear had not. For example, earlier we saw Aristotle arguing that rectilinear motion cannot be eternal, whereas circular motion could be; natural rectilinear motion took place only after a body had been moved violently from its natural place; and the circular motion of the heavenly spheres, continuing eternally in imitation of the immobility of the Prime Mover, was ultimately responsible for all other motions in the universe (and therefore of the violent motions presupposed by all natural rectilinear motion). And we shall soon see the fundamental role played by circular motion in ancient and medieval astronomy. For such reasons, it could easily appear that, if it came to a choice between rectilinear and circular impetus—or, more generally, between rectilinear and circular motion as a basis for physics—it was more plausible to choose the latter than the former. And indeed, it did so appear to Galileo in writing his *Dialogue Concerning the Two Chief World Systems*; and in the discussion of that work in chapter 4 below, the full force of the difficulty of this step will become abundantly apparent.

3. *The abandonment of the idea of impetus as an internal force distinct from the body and maintaining it at constant speed.* Again, the power of the Aristotelian dictum that all violent motion requires an extrinsic contact force, together with his arguments that rectilinear motion could not be eternal, stood in the way of this step. Both reason and experience, as we have seen, seemed fully behind Aristotle on these central points.

But there were other, more general problems too. Two types of objections, in addition to the preceding difficulties, also constituted barriers to an easy transition from Buridan's theory to modern physics: (a) objections within the Impetus tradition itself to Buridan's version of the concept; and (b) objections against the Impetus Theory from the general standpoint of Aristotelianism.

a. In holding that impetus is corrupted only through overcoming external counteragencies, did not Buridan ignore the natural tendency of the projected bodies themselves to resist motion—an *inclinatio ad quietem*, an inclination to come to rest, on the part of the body itself, so that *even in a void* the impetus would be corrupted in overcoming this *intrinsic* resistance of the body itself? On this view, a body, even in a void, would not continue to move forever under the influence of a rectilinear impetus, but would gradually decelerate as the quantity of impetus was reduced in overcoming the *inclinatio ad quietem* of the body. The *inclinatio ad quietem* view was held by Buridan's great successor at the University of Paris, Nicole Oresme, and perhaps by the majority of succeeding members of the Impetus tradition (though Benedetti held Buridan's view). (Another quite distinct view, sometimes attributed to Oresme, and apparently actually held by many Impetus Theorists, was that impetus is *self*-corrupting. On this view, even if there is no *inclinatio ad quietem*—and after all, the body inclines to rest only when it reaches its natural place—a body moving in a void would decelerate to a stop, because the impetus decays over time by its own nature. We shall therefore distinguish three versions of the Impetus Theory: the conserved impetus or Buridanian view, the *inclinatio ad quietem* or Oresmean view, and the self-corrupting impetus view.)

b. Although the Impetus Theory seems to us, as to Duhem, to have constituted a brilliant and profound advance, anticipating modern ideas three centuries before Galileo, it is not necessarily true that it seemed so at that time. It was only one of many deviant movements within the broad framework of Aristotelianism, not necessarily seen, by others than its adherents, as any more significant than any of the others. Indeed, there was abundant reason for thinking that it was perverse and wrong, when seen from that general framework within which even the Impetus Theorists themselves were working. For one thing, Buridan claimed impetus to be not a substance, a thing or a kind of stuff, but a form, and a mere accidental one at that (after all, violent motion is accidental). But accidents presuppose substances in which they inhere; and although they can change *in* that substance, is it possible literally to *transfer* an accident, a quality, from one substance to another? (One thing might *cause* another thing to change color, to actualize its potentiality with regard to that color; but in doing so, surely it does not literally transfer its own color, without any of its own matter, to that other thing.) Buridan seemed to rest his case on such a possibility; and after all, Aristotle himself had advocated the transmission of a "power" (a form of *some* kind) to account for the continuance of violent motion. Nevertheless, there was a strong tendency within the Aristotelian tradition to reject the doctrine of transmission of qualities from substance to substance.

Again, in supposing the quantity of impetus that can be conveyed to a body to be dependent on the quantity of matter in the body, Buridan seems also to have departed from fundamental Aristotelian principles without giving any particular justification for his deviation. For Aristotle, the forms which a body can potentially achieve or receive are not dependent on the (prime) *matter* of the body—matter is pure potentiality, and, considered merely as matter, can acquire *any* form. Rather, the potentiality to receive further forms is dependent on the forms already present in the body, and is limited by them. It thus made sense for Aristotle to hold that certain things are able by nature (i.e., because of their essential forms) to receive the "power of being a movent" while others cannot; and on yet other grounds, to argue that it was the intermediate elements, air and water, that possessed that capacity, not bodies made of fire and earth. Aristotle is arguing in this vein in the following rather obscure passage.

> The air is as it were instrumental to the force. For air is both light and heavy, and thus *qua* light produces upward motion, being propelled and set in motion by the force, and *qua* heavy produces a downward motion. In either case the force transmits the movement to the body by first, as it were, impregnating the air. That is why a body moved by constraint [i.e., violently] continues to move when that which gave the impulse ceases to accompany it. Otherwise, i.e., if the air were not endowed with this function, constrained movement would be impossible. (*On the Heavens*, 301b23–29)[10]

Finally, in making the quantity of impetus receivable depend on the "quantity of (prime) matter," Buridan seems to be speaking utter nonsense from an Aristotelian point of view. For matter—prime matter—is utterly formless, indeterminate, and, considered merely as matter, has no quantity.

Thus, contrary to our original impression, it may seem strange that the Impetus Theory enjoyed such a long career. Nevertheless, we must remember that Aristotle's position regarding the continuation of violent motion was a weak one: at best it was obscure, and left open the possibility of alternative interpretations; at worst it was wrong, and had to be replaced by a better alternative, even though that latter might ultimately require further adjustments or replacements—even, perhaps, some radical ones—elsewhere in the total Aristotelian system. (In view of the drastic modifications of the Aristotelian system that a full development of the Impetus Theory would seem to have required, one must wonder about the justice of calling it "Aristotelian," despite the many common features it shared with that philosophy.) The situation is not an uncommon one in the history of science: theories are rarely fully precise; more often, they leave open room for interpretation. They are rarely complete, usually leaving unexplained some facts which they ought to explain. And often there are facts which they seem, more or less definitely, to fail to explain.[11] The latter is the case here: Although the extent to which the Aristotelian system had failed in the present instance was debatable, the objection had to be taken seriously. And therefore, even though the Impetus Theory seemed to require more extensive overhauling of the prevailing system than it actually provided, it still deserved consideration and development. By the late sixteenth century it had spread from Paris to other parts of Europe, including Italy.

Shortly before Buridan proposed the Impetus Theory at the University of Paris, another fourteenth-century development of considerable importance was taking place at Merton College, Oxford. This work was begun by Thomas Bradwardine, who argued, in a most unAristotelian way, that

> it is [mathematics] which reveals every genuine truth, for it knows every hidden secret, and bears the key to every subtlety of letters; whoever, then, has the effrontery to study physics while neglecting mathematics, should know

from the start that he will never make his entry through the portals of wisdom. (Bradwardine, *Tractatus de continuo*; quoted in J. A. Weisheipl, "Galileo and His Precursors," in McMullin, *Galileo*, p. 94)

Bradwardine's most important substantive work concerned an attempt to modify the equation $V = F/R$. We saw that that law fails when F is less than R; and this was the particular objection which Bradwardine attempted to overcome. His own solution, which in modern notation may be expressed as $V = \log(F/R)$, is irrelevant to our purposes, and will not be examined here; but it is important in showing that alternatives—quantitative analyses of the relationship between speed, force, and resistance—were being considered. Another such alternative, also already considered in the Middle Ages, was adopted by Galileo in his early work, *On Motion*, which will be discussed in chapter 3.

Bradwardine's mathematical approach to the analysis of motion was continued at Merton College by John Dumbleton, Richard Swineshead, and William Heytesbury. These men attempted to give precise definitions of such concepts as uniform change or motion, "difform" change or motion (acceleration), and instantaneous speed; and in doing so they frequently arrived at mathematical notions which were quite sophisticated for the time. A change of place, for example, was defined as uniform when equal distances were covered in equal time-intervals, no matter how small; otherwise it was difform. The original statement of this definition was formerly attributed to the *Two New Sciences* of Galileo. Uniform difform motion (uniformly accelerated motion) could then be defined; Heytesbury in particular defined it as the "speed of a speed." The instantaneous speed of a body was defined as the speed of the uniform motion which would arise if, from that instant, the body were to continue to move in the same way.

This school was further responsible for the important "Mertonian Rule," or "Mean-Speed Theorem," regarding uniformly accelerated motion: that the distance traveled in a uniform difform motion in a given time is equal to the distance traveled in a uniform motion in the same time, and that the speed of that uniform motion is equal to the instantaneous speed of the uniformly difform motion at the middle instant of the time of travel. This rule found its way to Paris, where Oresme applied the graphing techniques which he invented to give a geometrical proof of it. It is important to note that the "odd-number rule"—that the distances traveled by a uniformly accelerating body in succeeding equal time-intervals are to each other as the odd numbers beginning with unity—and the law that the distance traveled by a body is proportional to the square of the time traveled, both follow from the Mertonian Rule. The Mertonians were aware of the first consequence, and Oresme was aware of both. It was with respect to these laws, and more specifically to the times-squared law, that Salviati, in Galileo's *Two Chief World Systems*, remarks that

> [there is a mathematical proof of this statement], and not only of this, but of many other beautiful properties belonging to natural motions and to projectiles also, all of which have been discovered and proved by our friend [i.e., Galileo]. I have seen and studied them all, to my very great delight and amazement, seeing a whole new science arise around a subject on which hundreds of books have been written; yet not a single one of the infinite admirable conclusions within this science had been observed and understood before our friend. (*Two Chief World Systems*, p. 222)

And earlier we saw Mach claiming for Galileo the original statement of these definitions and laws of mechanics. On the other hand, of course, the fact that the fourteenth-century writers stated these definitions and laws does not necessarily imply that Galileo got them from reading those men's works or those of any intermediaries.

Other relationships concerning motion were also considered. Albert of Saxony and others suggested, or at least implied, that, for uniformly accelerated motions, the speed was proportional to the distance traveled; others, including Oresme, maintained (correctly) that it was proportional to the time. However, as was mentioned earlier, the question of the compatibility or incompatibility of these two relationships does not seem to have been raised: as late as 1604, we will find Galileo himself claiming to deduce the latter from the former.

In assessing the contributions of these fourteenth-century thinkers, it is important to recognize the extent to which their analyses were conducted on a highly general and abstract level. In the first place, their analyses of uniform and difform motion or change were meant to apply to change *in general*—not merely locomotion (change of place), but also qualitative change (alteration) and quantitative change (growth and diminution). Thus the Mertonian Rule was meant to be a mean *degree* theorem, not just a mean *speed* theorem: in its most general form, it stated that a uniformly difform change of form (whether of quality, quantity, or position) corresponds to the middle degree of that changing form between the *terminus a quo* and the *terminus ad quem*. The very words, uni*form* and dif*form*, reveal the connection with the general Aristotelian doctrine of change: in difform motion, a further changing form is superimposed on the original one.

Secondly, there was little or no concern with applying their analyses to real cases—with pointing to examples of, say, uniform difform motion in the physical world. Rather, they were concerned with carrying out the logical implications of their definitions of "uniform motion," "difform motion," and so forth—with carrying out analyses of the hypothetical form, "*If* there were any such thing as uniform difform motions, then . . . ," rather than with saying that there are any such motions. Thus they nowhere explicitly state that their analysis of uniform difform motion applies to the case of falling or rising bodies; the first person actually to make this connection explicitly (for the case of falling bodies) was apparently Domingo de Soto in 1545. It would be a mistake, however, to conclude from this lofty indifference to specific applications that men like Oresme were *necessarily* unaware of the applicability of their analyses to the case of falling bodies: after all, Aristotle himself had declared the motion of falling bodies to be accelerated; and in any case, concentration on theoretical generality is no crime, and is a characteristic even of much scientific work today.

Our focus on the Mertonian and Parisian schools has neglected some other medieval developments which were, or which may well have been, important to the rise of modern science, and particularly to Galileo's thought. For reasons of space, we have ignored, for example, the important medieval developments in statics, which included detailed considerations of motion on an inclined plane, and which derived largely from the work of Jordanus Nemorarius in the thirteenth century; the nominalism of William of Ockham; and the development of the Aristotelian conception of scientific method, which was an important movement at the University of Padua in the years before Galileo's arrival there. Although the third of these developments will be referred to in chapter 4 below, we shall unfortunately have to pass over these and other interesting and important potential factors in the background of Galileo's work.

The Astronomical Background

When one watches the stars throughout the night, one finds them rising in the east, moving across the sky, and ultimately setting in the west (except for some stars which describe circular paths around the North Star without ever going below the horizon). This phenomenon can be explained in either of two ways (or some combination of both): either the stars are, as it were, attached to or embedded in a spherical shell which rotates from east to west once every twenty-four hours (roughly), carrying the stars around; or else the earth rotates in the same period from west to east. Aristotle rejected the possibility of the earth's rotation, or of its having any motion of any kind, except for the natural downward movement of pieces of earth removed from their natural place. Hence he concluded in favor of the first alternative: there is a "sphere of the fixed stars" which rotates once daily around the center of the universe (and therefore around the center of the earth, which coincides with that point).

As time proceeded, arguments against the rotation of the earth, and therefore in favor of the rotation of the sphere of the stars, were developed and elaborated. Of these, the following were the most important. (1) If the earth rotated, a terrific wind would be set up in the direction opposite that of the rotation, due to the earth's rotating beneath the place of air. (Analogously, as the earth rotated under the place of water, floods would be created.) (2) If the earth rotated from west to east, then an object dropped from a height would hit the ground at a point due west of the point directly beneath the dropping hand, because while the object was falling along a radius of the universe, the earth's rotation would carry the point originally beneath the hand in an eastward direction. (3) If the earth were in rapid rotation, everything that was not tied down would be thrown off, and perhaps the earth itself would fly apart. (This argument could not be transferred to the rotation of the outermost sphere by saying that its much more rapid rotation would cause it to fragment: for, as Aristotle had argued, the outermost sphere is not in any place; outside it is nothing, not even a void, into which it might fly apart. The deep implications of Aristotle's use of the concept of "place" rather than that of "space" are nowhere more evident than in this argument.)

The Impetus Theorists provided counterarguments to these contentions. (1) The earth, in rotating, communicates an impetus to the air, which impetus carries the air around along with the rotating earth, so that there is no wind. (2) The motion of the falling object is a composite of a downward motion caused by gravity and an eastward-directed motion due to the impetus conveyed to the object by the dropping hand, which is being carried around by the rotating earth. The composition of the two tendencies makes the object hit the ground at the point directly beneath the dropping hand despite the rotation of the earth.

Behind these first two Impetus counterarguments is a profound shift from Aristotelian views. Consider the second: Aristotelian physics had maintained that, on the hypothesis of the earth's rotation, once the hand (pushing the object along as the hand was moved from west to east by the rotating earth) was removed from the object, the latter's natural motion would automatically take over: it would move along a radius of the universe to its natural place. (This ignores any effects of the air on the motion of the falling object; but neither the Aristotelians nor the Impetus Theorists seem to have considered whether such effects would carry the object eastward from the radial line.) The conclusion would necessarily follow that the point on the earth's surface originally beneath the falling object would have moved eastward while the body was falling, so that by the time the latter hit the ground, a point westward of the original point would have rotated around to meet it. That is, *given the Aristotelian laws of motion, the additional premise of the earth's rotation would lead to a conclusion not borne out by observation*: for the object *does* hit the ground at the point directly beneath the dropping hand. *Therefore one of the premises which implied that it should hit the ground at a point west of that one—either the set of Aristotelian laws of motion, or the assertion of the earth's rotation—must be false.* The Aristotelians, not questioning the first, or even making it explicit in their argument, rejected the second. What the Impetus counterargument accomplished was to bring out the fact that the Aristotelian laws of motion underlie the argument as a hidden premise, and to show that an alternative to the Aristotelian laws could save the postulate of the earth's rotation: replacing the Aristotelian conception of motion by the Impetus conception in the argument, the latter together with the hypothesis of the earth's rotation lead to the conclusion that the object *would* hit the ground at the point directly beneath the dropping hand. This conclusion being borne out by observation, the hypothesis of the earth's rotation would be salvaged. (Inertial physics also has the object hitting the ground at the point beneath the dropping hand, but only approximately, for short distances of fall. Because the object traverses a greater arc in a given time at the top of its path than does the point at the bottom, the object will hit the ground at a point *eastward* of the point directly beneath; and because of "Coriolis forces" acting on the body if it is not located at the equator, the object will be displaced away from the direct east-west line as it falls.)

In the light of this discussion, it should not be surprising that Pierre Duhem, who rediscovered the Impetus Theory, argued in his great work on the philosophy of science, *The Aim and Structure of Physical Theory*, that there is no such thing as a crucial experiment—that any hypothesis may be salvaged in the face of any observational result by making appropriate changes elsewhere in the assumptions from which we argue. Other writers have gone even further, arguing that this case demonstrates how, at the root of scientific thought, there are certain very broad and basic ideas which while themselves not established or establishable by experience, govern the interpretation of experience. Thus the fact that the object hits the ground at the point directly beneath the dropping hand can either support or refute the hypothesis of the rotation of the earth, depending on the fundamental conception of motion assumed in the interpretation. The scientific revolution (or, more generally, the differences between Aristotelian, Impetus, and inertial physics) is then viewed not as arising out of the discovery of new facts, but as a shift in *viewpoint*. The transition from Aristotelian to inertial physics, according to this way of interpreting it, consisted not in a closer attention to facts (as older historians like Mach would have had it); rather it consisted in "handling the same bundle of data as before, but placing them in a new system of relations with one another by giving them a different framework, all of which virtually means putting on a different kind of thinking-cap" (Butterfield, *The Origins of Modern Science*, p. 1). Assuming, then, that Galileo was the founder or representative of a new physics, it was because he viewed old facts in a new way, according to this interpretation, rather than because he discovered new facts (or laws).

In any case, these Impetus counterarguments made possible the conception of a rotating earth. Oresme added to them the idea that the rotation of the earth would not be noticeable to us, because everything in our immediate surroundings shares that motion with us. This has been called —somewhat misleadingly, as we shall see later—the "principle of relativity." The Impetus arguments in favor of the possibility of the earth's rotation were repeated in the writings of both Copernicus and Galileo, along with the principle of relativity; indeed, the latter has come to be called, more specifically, the "principle of Galilean relativity."

As to the third argument against the possibility of the earth's rotation—namely, that such rotation would send unattached objects flying off, and would perhaps fragment the earth—Oresme countered it with a view which is essentially independent of the Impetus Theory. Returning to the doctrine of gravity presented in the *Timaeus* (62C–64A; Cornford, *Plato's Cosmology*, pp. 262–66), that like attracts like, Oresme argues that earthy objects will be held to a rotating earth by their natural attraction for earth. (This view, which was to be highly influential in the early seventeenth century, must not be confused with Newton's *universal* gravitation, according to which *all* bodies, and not only *like* bodies, attract one another.) Oresme's view makes gravity a relation between bodies and other bodies, not, as for the Aristotelian tradition, between bodies and places. It therefore dispenses with the need for unique places, and therefore, to *that* extent at least, with the requirement that the universe be finite in order to mark out such places. (It still, however, leaves untouched the Aristotelian contention that there can be no such thing as an actual infinite.) It also makes plausible the motion of the earth through space (rather than, as in the case of the previous arguments, merely its rotation *in* place), as defenders of Copernicanism were later quick to see. Oresme himself maintained that his conception of gravity was consistent with the existence of more than one world. In general, then, the Impetus Theory, together with Oresme's theory of gravity, provided a non-Aristotelian physics which made reasonable not only the earth's daily *rotation* on its axis, but also its annual *revolution* around the sun.

In addition to the motions of the stars, it was also necessary to give an account of the motions of the planets (including, for the Greeks and medievals, the sun and moon). Here, as before, we find the circle playing a fundamental role. The highly irregular motions of the planets could not be looked upon, as was the case with the stars, as due to their being embedded in a sphere of ether rotating uniformly around the center of the earth. Nevertheless, Plato laid down the requirement that *those irregular planetary paths be interpreted as due to a composition of uniform circular motions around a common center, the center of the universe.* Such a system of concentric spheres was developed by Eudoxus and Callipus, and further elaborated by Aristotle. Each planet was assigned a *set* of spheres, the planet being embedded in the innermost. The separate motions of the individual spheres in the set were all uniform; however, their different orientations and speeds made the *apparent* path of the planet against the background of the fixed stars irregular.

The Eudoxian-Aristotelian system, however, was not given a precise mathematical development, and the system that was ultimately adopted by working astronomers was the highly geometrized one devised by Ptolemy and others. According to the Ptolemaic system, the planet is located on a small circle (epicycle) rotating uniformly around a center located on a large circle (deferent) which in turn rotates uniformly around another center. (There could also be smaller epicycles on the original epicycles.)

Two further astronomical systems are important for our purposes. One, of course, is the Copernican, in which the moon revolves around the earth, the earth and the other planets revolve around the sun (located at the center of the universe), and the sphere of the stars remains stationary, with the earth rotating on its axis daily. The other is the Tychonic, devised by Tycho Brahe toward the end of the sixteenth century, and according to which the earth is stationary at the center of the universe, the moon and the sun go around the earth, and the planets go around the sun. (It will be remembered that Tycho's parallax measurements of the nova of 1572 and the comet of 1577 led him to reject the Aristotelian solid etherial spheres; and we have seen that, for once, Galileo agreed with the Danish astronomer on this point.) By the time of Galileo, many astronomers had abandoned the Ptolemaic in favor of the Tychonic system.

Fortunately, the technical details of these various systems are not relevant for our purposes: Galileo, in discussing the "two chief world systems," is hardly concerned at all with the relative technical merits of the Copernican as opposed to either the Aristotelian, Ptolemaic, or Tychonic system (the latter of which he totally ignores, despite the fact that, at the time, it was the "chief" world system competing with the Copernican). In order to understand the aims of Galileo in his *Dialogue Concerning the Two Chief World Systems*, it is necessary to examine a distinction that had been made since Greek times between two types of theories.

The Ptolemaic system did not abide faithfully by the Platonic requirements for an astronomical theory: the epicycles did not go around the center of the universe, and as a matter of fact neither did the deferents, which were off-center; further, the revolutions of the deferents were not uniform with respect to the center of the universe, nor even with respect to their own centers, but to a point off center. Further, since the epicycles jutted out on either side of the deferents, it seemed necessary to say either that they and the planets they carried had to plow through the solid ether of the adjoining spheres as their own deferents carried them around, or else that there were void spaces between the spheres to make room for the epicycle spheres. Neither of these alternatives seemed particularly palatable; and so a distinction grew up between a *physical* system of astronomy and a *mathematical one*. Many alleged that, because of the preceding flaws, the Ptolemaic system *could* not be a portrayal of the real structure of the universe: as Aristotle had argued, the earth *had* to be at the exact center of the universe, and *all* natural circular motion *had* to be "around the center." The Ptolemaic system was thus not only unfaithful to the Platonic requirements for an astronomical theory; more seriously, it was inconsistent with Aristotelian physics. Therefore it had to be considered as being a mere mathematical device, convenient for calculating planetary positions, but by no means constituting an account of physical reality. For the latter, one had to turn to the Aristotelian system (despite the fact that it seemed unable to account for variations in the brightness of planets as they progressed across the sky—a variation which strongly suggested a variation of distance from the earth).

Needless to say, this distinction between two types of astronomical theories—those which are mere calculating devices, "hypotheses," and those which are representative of the real structure of the universe—found a basis in Aristotle's view that quantity is a mere accident, irrelevant to the study of "nature." Of course the legitimacy of constructing astronomical theories divorced from physics was a matter of controversy during the Middle Ages, some arguing that Ptolemy's astronomy should not be used because it was incompatible with physics, while yet others tried to make it compatible with (Aristotle's) physics. Nevertheless, the distinction dominated the interpretation of astronomical theories; and in terms of it, Copernicanism *could* be viewed as a mere "hypothesis," not at all incompatible with Aristotelian physics (and therefore with Church doctrine), simply because it is irrelevant to "physics," that is, the study of real nature. And so it was interpreted by the anonymous author (Andreas Osiander) of the preface to Copernicus' book, *On the Revolution of the Heavenly Spheres* (1543). But Copernicus himself advanced arguments, taken from the Impetus tradition, in favor of the physical possibility of his system.

And so also did Galileo; and this is why he is minimally concerned with the technical details of any of the three rivals of the Copernican system. The opposition, for him, is at bottom not between that system and either the Aristotelian, the Ptolemaic, or the Tychonic; rather, it is between the view that the universe is *sun-centered* and the view that it is *earth-centered*, all three of the non-Copernican systems agreeing on the latter point. (This is why he can afford to ignore Tycho's system: because, in respect to this point, it is only a newer version of the old view.) The argument, then, is a *physical* one, not a mere *mathematical* one. Thus Sagredo asks:

Is not this the conclusion we are seeking to understand —whether it should be held with Aristotle and Ptolemy that the earth alone remains fixed in the center of the universe while all the celestial bodies move, or on the other hand that the stellar sphere remains fixed with the sun in its center, the earth being located elsewhere and having the motions which appear to be those of the sun and the fixed stars? (*Two Chief World Systems*, p. 129)

It is significant that these words are put in the mouth of Sagredo rather than of Galileo's mouthpiece Salviati; the latter cloaks his position with a thin veil of conformity with the instructions of the Church officials:

Before going further I must tell Sagredo that I act the part of Copernicus in our arguments and wear his mask. As to the internal effects upon me of the arguments which I produce in his favor, I want you to be guided not by what I say when we are in the heat of acting out our play, but after I have put off the costume, for perhaps then you shall find me different from what you saw of me on the stage. (*Two Chief World Systems*, p. 131)

Hardly convincing: Galileo—Salviati—is clearly concerned with presenting a powerful case in favor of the physical reality of the Copernican system of astronomy, a reality in which no reader could doubt that Galileo himself passionately believed. And the book can hardly be understood as less than a rejection of whatever elements of the old philosophy and physics were incompatible with that system, and a replacement of them by a new physics. In order to understand what that new physics was, and how much of the old it rejected, and what its relation to "modern" physics was, we must turn to the development of Galileo's ideas leading up to the mature thought of the *Two Chief World Systems* and ultimately the *Two New Sciences*.

3

The Early Development of Galileo's Thought

The Pisan Period

Galileo's *On Motion,* written about 1590 while he was at the University of Pisa, begins with a consideration of the heavy and the light: "All natural motion, whether upward or downward, is the result of the essential heaviness or lightness of the moving body" (p. 13). Two bodies are defined as equally heavy "which, when they are equal in size [i.e., in volume], are also equal in weight" (p. 13). Thus, heaviness is equated with weight per unit volume, or, in modern terms (with "mass" replacing "weight"), density or specific gravity. Galileo is in agreement with Aristotle that

> every day we observe with our senses that the places of the heavy are those which are closer to the center of the universe, and the places of the light those which are farther distant. Therefore we have no reason to doubt that such places have been determined for them by nature. (*On Motion,* p. 14)

Nevertheless, Galileo complains that

> no other reason for the existing arrangement is adduced by the philosophers [including Aristotle] than that everything must be disposed in some arrangement, and that it has pleased Providence on high to employ this arrangement. . . . Yet, if we look at the matter more carefully, surely we shall not have to conclude that nature was under no necessity in this arrangement, and obtained no advantage from it, and that she somehow operated solely according to whim and chance. (*On Motion,* pp. 14–15)

Such questions are characteristic of Galileo throughout his career: again and again we find him, even when he agrees with Aristotle, trying to get a deeper explanation. Thus in his *Two Chief World Systems*, he agrees with Aristotle on the importance of circles in the study of motion, and indeed goes further than the Philosopher in asserting this primacy; yet he ridicules the reasoning employed by Aristotle—the "perfection" of the circle—to explain that importance, and seeks to deduce it from deeper premises about the order of nature. So too, in *On Motion*, rather than stop with the facile "by nature" explanation of why heavy bodies tend to the center of the universe, Galileo

> anxiously sought from time to time to think of some cause, if not necessary, at least reasonable and useful. And, in truth, I have found that nature chose the existing arrangement with complete justice and with consummate wisdom. For if it is true, as ancient philosophers believed, that there is a single kind of matter in all bodies, and those bodies are heavier which enclose more particles of that matter in a narrower space, . . . then surely it was logical that bodies containing more matter in a narrower space should also occupy narrower places, such as are those that are nearer the center. (*On Motion*, p. 15)

That is, because there is less space near the center—or so Galileo argues—it is "logical" that denser bodies should naturally occupy them. The argument may seem strange to us; but it shows Galileo's dissatisfaction with Aristotelian explanations which tell us that things of a certain kind behave the way they do just because they *are* that way (that is their nature), and which fail to relate those "natures" in revealing ways to their surroundings, or to other kinds of things. The relationships which Galileo seeks do give such connections, and, furthermore, as in the present case, are often suggestive, at least, of quantitative relationships.

But the most interesting thing about these passages is not the way they go beyond Aristotle, but rather the ways in which they agree with him. Galileo reveals himself as believing still in the finiteness of the universe, with a definite central point marked out, and with sublunar bodies moving up or down to their appointed places; and although he gives, or seeks, deeper explanations of the "natures" of different sorts of bodies, which explanations make those natures appear reasonable, bodies still have natures which are responsible for the way they behave. Despite his search for explanations which go beyond the natures of specific kinds of things, Galileo's universe is still fundamentally Aristotelian.

Nevertheless, it is not long before we find another influence in Galileo's early thought—one which leads him beyond modification, deepening, and into more radical disagreements about details even while he remains faithful to the general conception. For Galileo soon announces and defends three major conclusions.

1. There is no such thing as a nature of "lightness": all bodies are heavy, and what is called lightness is only a lesser degree of heaviness. This point must have been one which he was coming to accept while writing *On Motion*; for whereas in the first version lightness and heaviness are sometimes distinguished as separate natures, the later versions ascribe heaviness to all bodies. However, the point does appear in the first version, more strongly in the later portions of the work, as in the following passage:

> The reason that fire does not move downward is not that fire has no weight, but that air, through which the fire would have to move, is heavier than fire. So too, the reason that air does not move downward is that it would have to move through water, and water, being heavier than air, does not permit this. Yet we must not say that air, just because it does not move downward, is entirely without weight. (*On Motion*, p. 61)

Bodies fall naturally, but they rise because they are displaced by heavier ones. Galileo will continue to accept this conclusion throughout his career.

2. The medium also has a natural heaviness, and bodies are displaced upward if they are less heavy (less dense) than the medium in which they are located; otherwise they

fall through the medium. If the body and the medium are equal in gravity, the body moves neither upward nor downward.

These two points show the extent—already apparent in *The Little Balance*—to which the work of "inimitable" or "peerless" Archimedes (*On Motion*, p. 103) had affected Galileo. Archimedes' *On Bodies in Water*, which had been printed in Latin at Venice in 1543 and translated into Italian by the mathematician Tartaglia in 1551, was based on the idea that a body in a fluid medium remains in equilibrium if its density (specific gravity) is equal to that of the medium; if it is denser than the medium, it sinks, and if the medium is denser than it, it rises. Thus Galileo's first two points are wholly Archimedean in spirit. However, there are two important ways in which Galileo's approach goes beyond that of the great Syracusan. First, Galileo puts the Archimedean analysis into the framework of the Aristotelian conception of the sublunar part of the universe, and applies it to the analysis of natural motion in general rather than to the behavior of bodies in a fluid. Such an application of Archimedean ideas is not at all odd: after all, Aristotle's realms of fire and air could be thought of as fluid media just as easily as water. Indeed, Benedetti had proposed just such a view shortly after Tartaglia's translation appeared, and we will see further similarities between Benedetti's approach and that of Galileo shortly. However, Galileo's work is more mathematical in orientation than Benedetti's.

The second respect in which Galileo goes beyond Archimedes stems from the fact that the latter's approach is basically *static*: although he does tell us the circumstances under which a body in a medium will rise or fall, those circumstances are analyzed in terms of departure from an equilibrium state. Galileo, however, focuses on *dynamic* aspects of the situation, holding that the greater the excess of the density (specific gravity) of the body over that of the medium, the faster it will fall through that medium; or conversely, the greater the excess of the density of the medium over that of the body, the faster the body will rise through it. Thus we arrive at Galileo's third major point.

3. The speed with which the body moves through the medium is proportional to the *difference* between the density of the body and that of the medium. That is, if V is the speed of the body, F its "heaviness" (density or specific gravity), and R the heaviness of the medium, Galileo's formula is:

$$V \propto (F-R)$$

We thus see yet another conception of the relationship between force, resistance, and speed—here applied to natural motion only—as well as an interpretation of how those concepts are to be applied (now, for example, the force, the "heaviness" or "gravity," is interpreted as density, not weight; and there is no natural lightness). The relationship $V \propto (F-R)$ had been considered during the Middle Ages by the Arab Avempace; Benedetti also held it, and there is no reason why he need have gotten it from any previous thinker: it is a straightforward development of Archimedean ideas, and we have seen that their application to problems of fall was a perfectly natural one to make.

The importance of the new formula was, however, great; for from it, as Galileo notes, "it can readily be seen that motion in a void does not have to be instantaneous" (*On Motion*, p. 47).

> The body will move in a void in the same way as in a plenum. For in a plenum the speed of motion of a body depends on the difference between its weight [i.e., its specific gravity or density] and the weight of the medium through which it moves. And likewise in a void its motion will depend on the difference between its own weight and that of the medium. But since the latter is zero, the difference between the weight of the body and the weight of the void will be the whole weight of the body. And therefore the speed of its motion [in the void] will depend on its own total weight. (*On Motion*, p. 45)

But not only is motion in a void now permitted, as it was not by the old $V \propto F/R$ formula; this new equation also implies that *bodies of different density will fall at different speeds in a void.* Every species of body has its own proper gravity—its specific gravity, or density; and it has a characteristic speed of fall in a void which depends solely on that specific gravity. Two balls of lead will fall at the same speed regardless of their weight, while a ball of lead will fall faster than a ball of wood, no matter what their weights. It is in this respect that Galileo claimed to be refuting Aristotle, who said (on the usual interpretation) that the speed of fall is proportional to the weight, so that heavier bodies fall faster than light ones regardless of density.

Galileo's view that the "heaviness" of a body—that is, its natural inclination to fall—is determined by its density or specific gravity rather than by its weight might even be understood as being *more* consistent with fundamental Aristotelian principles than was the view of Aristotle himself. For if "gravity" or "heaviness" is determined by the *nature* (or essence) of bodies, it must have to do with something which is *common* to all individuals of a certain *type* or *species*. But weight varies from individual to individual body; it is the density or specific gravity that is common to all bodies of the same kind. We must, of course, understand "types" or "kinds" here as species in the Aristotelian sense (Galileo says, "and let 'bodies of the same kind' be defined as those that are made of the same material, e.g., lead, wood, etc." [*On Motion*, p. 27]); but if we do, the interpretation of "heaviness" as "specific gravity" (gravity characteristic of the species) is more Aristotelian than Aristotle's own interpretation of it as (individual) weight. Galileo does not actually use such an argument, but it is clear that he easily could have.

Scholars, aware of Galileo's doctrine of *On Motion*, have long dismissed the story of the Leaning Tower of Pisa as a myth, invented by an adoring pupil, Vincenzio Viviani, after Galileo's death (and therefore more than half a century after the alleged event). According to that familiar story, Galileo is supposed to have dropped two objects (whether of different material or not) from the tower in 1589; their hitting the ground at the same time is alleged to have refuted "the philosophers" and to have ushered in the era of modern physics. We can see that the ideas Galileo was advocating at the time certainly did not imply that all bodies, regardless of material, fall at the same speed; quite the contrary, his view was that bodies of different material fall at different speeds. It was to be many years before Galileo would see that "in a medium totally devoid of resistance all bodies would fall at the same speed" (*Two New Sciences*, p. 69), and that neither the weight nor the density nor the composition of the body makes any difference to its speed of fall in a vacuum. And that was a truly new conception, which even Oresme and De Soto, for all their realization of the proportionality of speed and time in accelerated motion, did not understand.[1]

Meanwhile, *On Motion* posits, in effect, that as well as having a natural gravity, dependent on density, every kind of body, such as lead or wood, has a corresponding natural speed, which is the speed with which it would fall in a vacuum. All the medium does is to slow the body to a speed of fall less than the natural speed; and the amount of reduction is dependent on the density of the medium.

But this raises a difficult problem for Galileo: for it implies that in natural fall, the speed of the body should, like the density on which it depends, be *constant*. How, then, are we to account for the fact, known to Galileo, that freely falling bodies accelerate? In order to answer this question, Galileo introduces a theory of projectile (violent) motion. He asks us to consider the case of a heavy body thrown upward. A "motive force," he tells us,

is impressed by the projector upon the projectile. . . . It is a taking away of heaviness when the body is hurled upward, and a taking away of lightness, when the body is hurled downward. . . . Motive force, that is to say lightness [in the case of the body hurled upward], is preserved in the stone, when the mover is no longer in contact. . . . The impressed force gradually diminishes in the projectile when it is no longer in contact with the projector. (*On Motion*, pp. 78–79)

Galileo has adopted, then, the self-corrupting version of the Impetus Theory. (He explicitly rejects the Oresmean, or *inclinatio ad quietem*, version: "Nor is there any validity in the assumption made by [certain] writers, namely, a two-fold resistance to the motion of the body—one external, resulting from the density of the medium, the other internal, by reason of the determinate weight of the body" [*On Motion*, p. 49].[2]) When the object is thrown upward, the "lightness" conveyed to it is greater than the heaviness of the body, and so the body continues to rise after the throwing hand releases it. But, just as the heat of a body diminishes gradually after the heater has been withdrawn from it, and just as the sound of a bell diminishes when the striking hammer is no longer in contact with it, so also does this "impressed force" diminish gradually. As long, however, as the impressed lightness exceeds the natural gravity of the body, the latter will continue to rise, though ever more slowly as the quantity of impressed lightness diminishes; finally, the lightness becomes exceeded by the gravity, and the body begins to fall, with increasing speed as the lightness continues to decay:

> As the impressed force characteristically continues to decrease, the weight of the body begins to be predominant, and consequently the body begins to fall. Yet there still remains, at the beginning of this descent, a considerable force that impels the body upwards, which constitutes lightness, though this force is no longer greater than the heaviness of the body. For this reason the essential weight of the body is diminished by this lightness and consequently the motion is slower at the beginning. Furthermore, since the external force continues to be weakened, the weight of the body, being offset by diminishing resistance, is increased, and the body moves faster and faster. (*On Motion*, p. 89)

Thus acceleration is a violent imposition, "contrary to nature and accidental" (*On Motion*, p. 88), on the naturally constant speed of falling bodies.

It is with regard to his explanation of acceleration that Galileo departs most significantly from the views of Benedetti. The latter, as we have seen, held that all bodies are heavy, that the speed of a falling body is proportional to the difference of its density and that of the medium, and therefore that bodies of different densities will fall at different speeds in the same medium or in a void. On these points, there is agreement between Benedetti and Galileo, whether or not the latter was influenced, in *On Motion*, by the former. (Whether Galileo had heard of Benedetti and his views at the time of writing *On Motion* is debatable; see Stillman Drake's introduction to Drake and Drabkin, *Mechanics in Sixteenth-Century Italy*, pp. 36–41.) However, Benedetti maintained Buridan's version of the Impetus Theory, namely that impetus is diminished only through overcoming external resistances and counterforces. (Benedetti departed from Buridan, however, in admitting only rectilinear, and not circular, impetus.) He therefore explained acceleration of falling bodies in terms of successive accumulations of impetus by the falling body. His view therefore implies that the acceleration will continue to increase as long as the body falls.

Galileo's view, however, does not: for him, once the impressed force has diminished to zero, the body will fall the rest of the way at constant speed.

> Such acceleration must finally cease. For since the [motion of the] body is accelerated because the contrary [i.e., upward] force is continuously diminishing while [in consequence] the natural weight is being attained, it will stand to reason that the whole contrary force will finally be lost and the natural weight resumed, and, therefore, that acceleration will cease since its cause has been removed. (*On Motion*, p. 100)

Is there any evidence favoring this view? Yes, says Galileo: since a heavy body receives more impressed force than a less heavy one, it will take longer for the former to lose all its impressed force and assume a constant speed of fall. Indeed, the heights to which we are able to raise and then drop heavy objects are always too small for the impressed force to be used up, and so in such cases we never observe the stage of constant speed. Light bodies, on the other hand, do lose their lesser impressed force quickly enough, and provide evidence for the existence of a constant speed phase.[3]

Galileo's first systematic view of mechanics, as expressed

in *On Motion*, is, then, a synthesis of the following elements from his intellectual background:

Aristotle
1. The general Aristotelian picture of the universe.
2. The view that all violent motion requires an extrinsic contact force.

Archimedes
1. Hydrostatics, (a) extended from the behavior of bodies in water to the more general Aristotelian context of the analysis of natural fall of bodies in media, whether of fire, air, or water; and (b) given a dynamical application in a relationship between natural (specific) gravity and speed of fall.
2. Use of mathematics, facilitated by the precise definitions made possible by his Archimedean analysis of fall.

Self-corrupting Impetus Theory

Surely, then, there is no basis for the claim that "When reading his first utterances in the writings *De Motu* [*On Motion*] . . . one may imagine oneself transferred to Buridan's lecture room" (Dijksterhuis, *The Mechanization of the World Picture*, p. 334)! Nor is it accurate to say that in this work "the path he followed in the examination of motion lay completely outside the Aristotelian scheme of things" (Geymonat, *Galileo Galilei*, p. 12).

The Paduan Period

With the exception of some later interpolations, such as the reference to the parabolic trajectory of a projectile at the beginning of the Third Day, the results included in the latter portions of the First Day and the entirety of the Third Day of Galileo's *Two New Sciences* had been achieved before he left Padua in 1610. The most important of these substantive conclusions are the law that the distance travelled by a naturally falling body is proportional to the square of the time of fall, and the law that all bodies fall at the same speed in a vacuum. Particularly important for our present purposes are the opening pages of the Third Day. After giving a definition of uniform motion, Galileo proceeds to a discussion of naturally accelerated motion: "A motion is said to be uniformly accelerated, when starting from rest, it acquires, during equal time-intervals, equal increments of speed" (*Two New Sciences*, p. 155). Recognizing as it does the dependence of speed on time rather than on distance, this definition is substantially the same as that of the Mertonians. Theorem I, Proposition I, is the Mean Speed Theorem (Merton Rule): "The time in which any space is traversed by a body starting from rest and uniformly accelerated is equal to the time in which that same space would be traversed by the same body moving at a uniform speed whose value is the mean of the highest speed and the speed just before acceleration began" (*Two New Sciences*, p. 166). The proof is essentially the same as Oresme's. Theorem II, Proposition II, is the times-squared law: "The spaces described by a body falling from rest with a uniformly accelerated motion are to each other as the squares of the time-intervals employed in traversing these distances" (*Two New Sciences*, p. 167). The odd-number rule is given as Corollary I to this theorem. The entire discussion is interspersed with references to the behavior of the pendulum and of bodies moving down inclined planes.

It is clear, therefore, that sometime between the completion of *On Motion* in 1590 or shortly thereafter and his construction of the telescope and consequent shift of attention to astronomical issues, Galileo's ideas on mechanics underwent a drastic revision. How did this shift come about? That is, what were the considerations that led him to reject the views of *On Motion* and to accept these new conclusions? (The considerations leading him to reject his older views and those leading him to adopt the newer ones, of course, need not have been identical.)

The first indication of a change in Galileo's thinking about natural fall comes in 1604, the date of a letter to Paolo Sarpi and also the date assigned to a single-page manuscript having to do with the subject of that letter. In those documents, Galileo subscribes to the view that "the spaces passed by a naturally falling body are in squared proportion to the times, and consequently the spaces passed in equal times are as the odd numbers from one" (quoted in

Drake, "Galileo's Fragment on Falling Bodies," p. 341). In the letter Galileo tells Sarpi of his search for a proof of these propositions (and particularly of the former, since the latter is an immediate corollary of it).

> Thinking again about the matters of motion, in which to demonstrate the accidents observed by me, I lacked a completely indubitable principle to put as an axiom, I settled on a proposition which seemed quite natural and obvious; and with this assumed, I then demonstrate the rest. . . . And the principle is this: that the natural movable goes increasing in speed with that proportion with which it departs from the beginning of its motion. (Drake, "Galileo's Fragment," pp. 340–41)[4]

The principle is given a clearer statement in the fragment:

> I suppose (and perhaps I shall be able to demonstrate this) that the naturally falling body goes continually increasing its velocity according as the distance increases from the point from which it parted. (Drake, "Galileo's Fragment," p. 342)

Galileo's claim—and he offers a proof—is that the relationship $s \propto t^2$ can be deduced from the proposition $v \propto s$. We have seen earlier that these two propositions were proposed by a number of medieval thinkers, along with the proposition that the speed is proportional to the *time* fallen; and there is no evidence that those thinkers saw any conflict between the $v \propto s$ relationship and the other two. Nevertheless, the latter two are correct and the former is not: the true relationship is one of proportionality between speed and *time* ($v = at$); as for the distance fallen, the speed is proportional not to it, but to its square root ($v = (2as)^{1/2}$). Galileo's argument is thus an attempt to deduce a true conclusion from a premise which is in fact false.

We need not enter here into the vexed question of whether Galileo's deduction is erroneous. (Logicians distinguish between the *truth or falsity* of *propositions* and the *validity or invalidity* of *arguments*, and point out that a deductive argument from false premises to a true conclusion *can* be logically impeccable, that is, valid.) Nor need we inquire as to why, if the argument is invalid, Galileo failed for some years to see his error, or why he failed to see the falsity of his premise. (Drake's educated conjecture dates these events as occurring in 1609 or shortly thereafter.) The reason we can ignore these questions is that, as is clear from the letter and the fragment, Galileo was convinced of the truth of the times-squared relationship on grounds *independent* of the $v \propto s$ relationship and the deduction of the former from the latter. Indeed, his search for a proof clearly came *after* his conviction of the truth of the conclusion, of which he was more firmly convinced than he was of the premise from which he attempted to derive it.

We are left, then, with the question of how he arrived at the correct relationship. Three major possibilities have been defended.

1. That Galileo became acquainted with the relationship through sources growing out of the Mertonian tradition and Oresme (though of course he may not have read their works directly). Alternatively, he might be supposed to have become acquainted with the Merton Rule, and was able to deduce the $s \propto t^2$ relationship from it.

It might be supposed that this interpretation receives support from the parallels noted above between the definitions, theorems, and proofs given in the Third Day of *Two New Sciences* and those given by the Mertonians and Oresme. However, there is perhaps stronger reason to believe that, whatever the source of the arguments which he ultimately used in his finished presentation, his *coming to believe* in the $s \propto t^2$ relationship had nothing to do with Mertonian or Oresmean influences, direct or indirect. These considerations are the following.

It is true that there is evidence that Galileo may have become acquainted with the Merton Rule in his student days; but then he may not have remembered it (Galileo was apparently not a very conscientious student), and even if he did, he could not have put much stock in it, since he did not accept it or the $s \propto t^2$ relationship in *On Motion*. Further, if he was acquainted with the Merton Rule, why did he not use it as the axiom from which to deduce the $s \propto t^2$ relationship (as Oresme had done, and as Galileo himself would do in

Two New Sciences) instead of the $v \propto s$ relationship? For the proof on the basis of the Merton Rule is easy and straightforward. (Indeed, if he is supposed to have been acquainted with the rule and the relationship, should we not expect that he might also have been acquainted with the proof?) On the other hand, if he merely became acquainted with the relationship, without the Merton Rule, the problem still remains as to why he adopted it in 1604. Thus the hypothesis that he knew of the relationship, or of the rule from which it is deducible, fails to explain why he accepted $s \propto t^2$ as correct.

2. That he arrived at the relationship by generalization from experiments with pendulums and inclined planes. This is the interpretation suggested by Mach; and certainly it, too, seems strongly supported by Galileo's own references to such experiments in the Third Day of *Two New Sciences*. Nevertheless, historians of science have learned not to take such statements by scientists at face value. Thomas Settle summarizes such suspicions very concisely:

> There is no indication that Galileo had any intention in the Third Day of describing the actual sequence of steps he had followed, no indication that he had any other purpose in mind than providing a systematic and convincing exposition of his *finished* work, with the scaffolding removed and the debris of construction discarded. The two criteria of deductive rigor and clarity of exposition govern the sequence and these are in nowise dependent upon the chronology of discovery. (Settle, "Galileo's Use of Experiment as a Tool of Investigation," in McMullin, *Galileo*, p. 317)

Those who have rejected the experimentalist interpretation of the origin of Galileo's "modern" views have always had to appeal to this sort of argument in order to explain away the references to experiment in *Two New Sciences*. Those references are then interpreted as having had to do with *corroboration* or *illustration* of a law which had been *arrived at* prior to and independently of experiment. What is at issue here are two different versions of "empiricism": on the one hand, the *inductivist* version, according to which observations or experiments are made, and on the basis of these, generalizations (or laws or theories) are arrived at; and on the other hand, the *hypothetico-deductive* version, according to which the generalization (or law or theory) is arrived at first and the observations or experiments are made *subsequently* in order to confirm or falsify it. This distinction between two general types of "empiricist" interpretations of science will prove useful in chapter 5.

Despite his suspicion of Galileo's references to experiment in *Two New Sciences*, Settle himself accepts the experimentalist interpretation, and in the inductivist version.

> An excellent case can be made for saying that Galileo began his empirical investigations into this problem [of free fall] as early as the time of his Pisan professorship, 1589–1592, that these led him to perfect the inclined plane as a research tool, and that this in turn provided the data from which he constructed part of the Second Science [mechanics] of the *Discorsi*. (Settle, in McMullin, *Galileo*, p. 316)

Settle's own account supposes that Galileo became dissatisfied with the theory of *On Motion* because "there was no clear experimental instance in which a freely moving body had lost its retarding impressed power, and was proceeding at a uniform speed" (Settle, in McMullin, p. 320). McMullin likewise holds that "it would not be too difficult [for Galileo] to abandon the central thesis of the *De Motu*, the constancy of the velocity of free fall, since he had been entirely unable to find direct evidence in its support" (McMullin, "Introduction" to *Galileo*, p. 11). However, we have seen that Galileo *did* think he had evidence for his view, namely, in the behavior of very light falling bodies. If Galileo was set to experimenting in search of a new law by the failure of his Pisan theory, his reasons for rejecting the latter must have been more complex than that adduced by Settle and McMullin.

Stillman Drake is another defender of the possibility that Galileo arrived at the law of falling bodies by experiment.

> I do not mean [that he arrived at the law] by elaborate experiments such as those he later [in *Two New Sciences*]

described as having performed to corroborate the rules. It would be grossly anachronistic, both with respect to the history of experimental physics and with respect to the known procedures of Galileo, to assume that he reached the mathematical law of fall by carefully controlled measurements of falling bodies. That he confirmed the law in that way is virtually certain. But he could have arrived at it indirectly in a much simpler and more plausible way.

The times-squared law follows immediately from the odd-number rule for successive spaces in equal times.[5] . . . in 1602 Galileo was making observations that led him to recognize the continuing character of acceleration. A crude and hence plausible way in which he could have confirmed that would be to allow a heavy ball to roll a considerable distance over any convenient smooth slope, such as a paved ramp. In order to find out whether the ball continued to accelerate, he would have only to mark its place after equal times—say pulse-beats—and compare the distances between marks. In that way the approximate 1-3-5-7 relationship between marks might have been noted, from which the square law would be evident to any mathematician of the time. (Drake, *Galileo Studies*, p. 218)[6]

Other writers, however, have questioned whether the degree of instrumental and observational accuracy available to Galileo would have sufficed for the extraction of such a generalization from experiment. Those writers deny an experimental origin of the law, turning to a radically different interpretation.

3. That Galileo arrived at the law of falling bodies by some process of pure reasoning, independent of either historical sources or experiments. (The experiments reported in *Two New Sciences* are explained in the manner noted above: as corroborative rather than originative, or as illustrative rather than suggestive; in some cases, too, they are dismissed as "thought experiments," not really having been performed.)

Without necessarily committing himself to it, Drake proposes such a possibility.

A purely logical approach was also [in addition to the empirical one described above] accessible to Galileo. If the spaces traversed in free fall grow uniformly, they form an arithmetic progression. It would, however, be a special kind of progression, in which the sum of the first two terms must be in the same ratio to the sum of the second two terms as the first term is to the second, and the sum of the first three must be in this same ratio to the second three, and so on, since we could have taken the double or triple (and so on) of whatever we took for the first arbitrary space. If one then asks whether such a progression exists, one finds it almost immediately. It is not 1-2-3-4, because 3 plus 4 is not double 1 plus 2. But it is 1-3-5-7, the very next progression to be tried, because 5 plus 7 is three times 1 plus 3. Moreover, no other arithmetic progression will fulfill the condition. (Drake, *Galileo Studies*, pp. 218–19)

But the premise of Drake's suggestion is unfounded: in *On Motion*, at least, Galileo did not believe that all natural acceleration was uniform; "at the beginning of their natural motion, bodies that are less heavy move more swiftly than heavier ones" (*On Motion*, p. 106). This interpretation of Drake's presupposes that in the intervening period Galileo had abandoned this view in favor of the uniformity of acceleration; and that change remains to be explained.

But Drake merely suggests, without advocating, this non-experimental possibility in the case of the law of falling bodies. The most important defender of the general thesis that Galileo's modern science has a rational rather than an empirical origin is Alexandre Koyré. "It is thought," according to Koyré, "pure unadulterated thought, and not experience or sense-perception, as until then [i.e., with the Aristotelian tradition], that gives the basis for the 'new science' of Galileo Galilei" (Koyré, *Metaphysics and Measurement*, p. 13). He further states:

I should like to claim for him the glory and merit of having known how to dispense with experiments (shown to be nowise indispensable by the very fact of his having been able to dispense with them); yet the experiments were unrealizable in practice with the facilities at his disposal. (Koyré, *Metaphysics and Measurement*, p. 75)

In opposition to this last point, Settle has tried to reconstruct and perform Galileo's own experiments, following his descriptions of the construction of the plane faithfully, and carrying out the observations in no more sophisticated ways than would have been available to Galileo. On the basis of this "experiment in the history of science," Settle concludes, contrary to Koyré's contention, that Galileo *could* have obtained the law by such experiments. But since Koyré's view, and more generally the question of the roles of reason and experiment in Galileo's thought, is the subject of chapter 5, we will postpone further discussion of it until then.

The importance of the controversy between these three alternative interpretations of the sources of Galileo's correct law of falling bodies must be recognized: for each of the three possibilities lends credence to a different interpretation of the rise of modern science. The first view, that the ideas were transmitted to Galileo from a medieval tradition, suggests that there was no "scientific revolution"; rather, modern science developed by a continuous transition out of Greek and medieval philosophy. The second and third views lend support, respectively, to empiricist and rationalist interpretations of the scientific revolution, and therefore can also be used to support such interpretations of the nature of science in general. And although the historical record is too scanty and inconclusive to enable us to decide between those alternatives on purely historical grounds, we can at least, while being faithful to what there is of the historical record, disentangle some of the philosophical issues involved.

But before proceeding to that discussion in chapter 5, we must first turn to the other great Galilean contribution to mechanics, the principle of inertia, and examine the extent to which Galileo adhered to it, and, to the extent that he did so, what the basis or source of that adherence was.

4

Galileo and the Principle of Inertia

A vast range of topics is taken up by Galileo in the *Dialogue Concerning the Two Chief World Systems*. Our interest here, however, will be in the extent to which he adheres in that work to the principle of inertia in its modern form (later in the chapter we will examine the role of that principle in *Two New Sciences*). We will find that his conception of "inertia," though it has some features in common with the modern conception, is far from being an achievement of the latter, and in some ways can be seen as a culmination of traditional ideas. In order to establish this, we will begin by focusing attention on five main points in the *Dialogue* which Galileo, through his spokesman Salviati, tries to establish.

PROPOSITION 1. *Anything but rest or circular motion is contrary to the orderliness of the universe.* Very early in the book, Salviati asserts his agreement with a basic contention of Aristotle, that the universe is fundamentally orderly:

> In [Aristotle's] conclusions up to this point I agree with him, and I admit that the world is a body endowed with all the dimensions and therefore most perfect. And I add that as such it is of necessity most orderly, having its parts disposed in the highest and most perfect order among themselves. (*Two Chief World Systems*, p. 19)

A perfect universe, one created by a benevolent and omnipotent God, is one which is necessarily ordered. But we must be careful to note that the kind of orderliness that is being agreed upon has to do with everything being located in its proper place: the "orderliness" in question is conceived on the analogy of the neatness or proper arrangement of a person's room, or of a well-planned city; and furthermore, there is only *one* arrangement that can be considered "neat." This conception of order is fundamentally different from that of later science, for which "the order of nature" consists, not of everything being in its appropriate place, but rather in obedience to laws. For that later conception, the concept of spatial location is irrelevant, indifferent to that of order: the spatial location of things has nothing to do with the orderliness—not the law-abidingness, not the neatness—of nature. We shall return to this important change later.

The concept of orderliness as proper positional arrangement of things is intimately connected with the Aristotelian idea that rest is the appropriate or "natural" condition of things: if the natural and proper state of things is a particular arrangement, then that proper condition would be upset by any motion which removes things from that arrangement. Hence any motion in a straight line, for example, would lead to the disturbance or destruction of orderliness. The preservation of order thus implies the "naturalness" of the condition of rest. (Remember that the natural straight-line motion of the elements always presupposed a violent motion which had moved the element out of its natural resting-place.) On the other hand, circular motion was considered admissible for classical thought, inasmuch as it leaves the body "in place": "a revolving sphere, while it is in motion, is also in a sense at rest, for it continues to occupy the same place" (Aristotle, *Physics*, 265b1–2). Galileo, while agreeing with this permissibility of circular motion in an ordered universe, extends the notion from *rotation* of a single body in place to include also the *revolution* of one body around another.

> Motion in a straight line could be of no use to the well-ordered parts of the world. We went on to say that the same did not hold of circular motions, of which the one made by the moving body upon itself keeps it ever in the same place, and the one which carries the moving body along the circumference of a circle about a fixed center puts neither it nor those about it in disorder, for such motion is finite and determinate. . . . [the body leaves] everything else inside and outside of [the circumference]

free for the use of others without impeding or disordering them. (*Two Chief World Systems*, p. 31)

(One must wonder: could there not still be collisions between bodies revolving around others? And does this not leave open the possibility that revolution of a body around a center, as opposed to rotation of a body on its own axis, could lead to the destruction of "order"?)

The fundamentality of rest or of circular motion, which appeared as a basic assumption of Aristotelian physics, is thus *deduced* by Galileo ultimately from a deeper assumption, namely that the world is perfect, and more immediately from a corollary of that assumption, namely that the universe is ordered. And his claim is that a consistent development of that fundamental assumption would lead to *the universality of circular motion as natural not only in the heavens but also in the sublunar domain, and hence to the denial of straight-line motion as natural even in the latter region.* In this respect, at least, far from rejecting all of classical thought, Galileo claims to be carrying out more consistently some of its deepest assumptions.

In an ordered universe, therefore, the only kind of order-preserving motion that is allowable is circular motion:

> After their optimum distribution and arrangement it is impossible that there should remain in [bodies] natural inclinations to move any more in straight motions, from which nothing would now follow but their removal from their proper and natural places; which is to say, their disordering.
>
> We may therefore say that straight motion serves to transport materials for the construction of a work; but this, once constructed, is to rest immovable—or, if movable, is to move only circularly. (*Two Chief World Systems*, p. 20)

PROPOSITION 2. *Natural circular motion is uniform and perpetual.* Here again we find Salviati agreeing with a classical assumption about natural motion; but again, we find him in an attempt to deduce this characteristic from more fundamental notions. His argument is as follows:

There is no point in the circumference which is not a first as well as a last point in the rotation. . . . This being the motion that makes the moving body continually leave and continually arrive at the end, it alone can be essentially uniform. For acceleration occurs in a moving body when it is approaching the point toward which it has a tendency, and retardation occurs because of its reluctance to leave and go away from that point; and since in circular motion the moving body is continually going away from and approaching its natural terminus, the repulsion and the inclination are always of equal strengths in it. This equality gives rise to a speed which is neither retarded nor accelerated; that is, a uniformity of motion. (*Two Chief World Systems*, pp. 31–32; the argument might easily occur to anyone who read the somewhat related discussion in Aristotle, *Physics*, 265a29 ff.)

Salviati continues by arguing that such motion will also be perpetual:

From this uniformity, and from the motion being finite [i.e., closed and cyclic], then follows its perpetual continuation by a successive repetition of rotations, which cannot exist naturally along an unbounded line or in a motion continually accelerated or retarded. I say "naturally," because straight motion which is retarded is forced motion, which cannot be perpetual, while accelerated motion arrives necessarily at an end if there is one. And if none exists, there cannot be motion toward it, for nature does not move whither it is impossible to arrive. (*Two Chief World Systems*, p. 32)

This last argument brings out the depth to which Aristotelian ideas still pervade Galileo's (or at least Salviati's) arguments here. Two such ideas in particular stand out: the idea that only the natural can be perpetual, anything forced necessarily coming to an eventual end; and the idea, implicit already in the view that the universe is perfectly ordered, that (to use Aristotle's own words) "nature does nothing in vain," such as, for example, to "move whither it is impossible to arrive." The universe is a product of intelligent design. Indeed, Galileo's arguments here are often reminiscent of those of Aristotle in *Physics*, book VIII, chapters 8 and 9, wherein the Philosopher argues that:

> The straight line traversed in rectilinear motion cannot be infinite: for there is no such thing as an infinite straight line; and even if there were, it would not be traversed by anything in motion; for the impossible does not happen and it is impossible to traverse an infinite distance. . . . rotary motion can be eternal: but no other motion, whether locomotion or motion of any other kind, can be so. (*Physics*, 265a17–26)

Natural motion presupposes the existence of contraries; and an infinite straight-line motion would have no *terminus ad quem*. Hence indefinite rectilinear motion cannot be natural.

PROPOSITION 3. *The only purpose that might possibly be attributed to straight-line motion is that it could be used to create or restore orderliness.*

The straight-line motion which Aristotle took as "natural" in the sublunar domain has thus been rejected: assuming that the basic natural tendency of bodies is to a state of order, "after their optimum distribution and arrangement it is impossible that there should remain in them natural inclinations to move any more in straight motions" (*Two Chief World Systems*, p. 20). Still, might it not be claimed that there is *some* role or purpose for such motion? Could it not be justified as "natural" in at least a derivative sense, as being instrumental in either (a) producing an original order, or (b) restoring an order which has somehow been disturbed? (Aristotle's natural rectilinear motions could, indeed, be looked on in the latter sense.) As to the former sense, the possibility of using straight-line motion to produce an original order,

> someone might say nevertheless that although a straight line (and consequently the motion along it) can be extended *in infinitum* (that is to say, is unending), still nature has, so to speak, arbitrarily assigned to it some terminus, and has given her natural bodies natural instincts to move toward that. And I shall reply that this might perhaps be fabled to have occurred in primordial chaos, where vague substances wandered confusedly in

disorder, to regulate which nature would very properly have used straight motions. By means of these, just as well-arranged bodies would become disordered in moving, so those which were previously badly disposed might be arranged in order. (*Two Chief World Systems*, pp. 19–20)

And so we might wish to say

with Plato that these world bodies, after their creation and the establishment of the whole, were for a certain time set in straight motion by their Maker. Then later, reaching certain definite places, they were set in rotation one by one, passing from straight to circular motion, and have ever since been preserved and maintained in this. A sublime concept, and worthy indeed of Plato. (*Two Chief World Systems*, p. 20)

(That, and how, the straight-line motion would produce the desired speed, is argued in what we have called propositions 4 and 5, below, as the uniformity and perpetuity of the circular motions produced have been established above, in proposition 2. We shall return to this "Platonic" concept shortly.)

Alternatively, straight-line motion *could* function (whether it does or not will be examined shortly) to *restore* an order which has been disturbed:

There is no doubt that to maintain the optimum placement and perfect order of the parts of the universe as to local motion, nothing will do but circular motion or rest. As to motion in a straight line, I do not see how it can be of use for anything except to restore to their natural location such integral bodies as have been accidentally removed and separated from their whole. (*Two Chief World Systems*, p. 45)

Aristotle's claim of the naturalness of straight-line motion, even in the sublunar domain, could be maintained consistently with the principle of the orderliness of the universe only by giving it a status subsidiary to the naturalness of circular motion. And this is the very *best* that could be said in favor of the naturalness of straight-line motion. Such is the argument of the man to whom has been attributed the discovery of the principle of inertia!

PROPOSITION 4. *If non-circular order-restoring motion does indeed exist, it would be accelerated and rectilinear.* This point is made in the context of the discussion of the "Platonic" theory of the origin of order. Salviati begins the argument by claiming that

> Every body constituted in a state of rest but naturally capable of motion will move when set at liberty only if it has a natural tendency toward some particular place; for if it were indifferent to all places it would remain at rest, having no more cause to move one way rather than another. Having such a tendency, it naturally follows that in its motion it will be continually accelerating. (*Two Chief World Systems*, p. 20)

Notice that this argument is not restricted to the acceleration of *falling* bodies, and that it is based, not on observational fact, but on fundamental ideas about "natural tendencies" toward places and about "indifference" to motion. The former idea is of course an Aristotelian one; the latter has a long and complex history; it is often, in a generalized form, referred to as the "Principle of Indifference"; Leibniz, making it a central tenet of his philosophy, referred to it more positively as the "Principle of Sufficient Reason."

It is not clear whether Galileo thinks that the conclusion of this passage "naturally follows" from the earlier part of the quotation. Certainly the conclusion *does not* follow, whether Galileo thinks it does or not: even if a body has a natural tendency toward a particular place, why should it not approach it with a speed that is uniform, or becomes so, or decreases? Perhaps hidden beneath his argument is the old—and disputed—idea that bodies get (so to speak) excited as they approach their goal, and so speed up. But if this is what he has in mind, Galileo is only *assuming* what he sets out to prove. On the other hand, perhaps he means the sentences *following* this statement of the conclusion to fill in the proof. The trouble is, as we shall see, they do not succeed. The sentences in question are:

> Beginning with the slowest motion, it will never acquire
> any degree of speed without first having passed through
> all the gradations of lesser speed—or should I say of
> greater slowness? For, leaving a state of rest, which is the
> infinite degree of slowness, there is no way whatever for
> it to enter into a definite degree of speed before having
> entered into a lesser, and another still less before that. It
> seems much more reasonable for it to pass first through
> those degrees nearest to that from which it set out, and
> from this to those farther on. (*Two Chief World Systems*,
> p. 20)

Again, the argument appeals, not to observed facts of motion, but to what Leibniz will later christen "The Principle
of Continuity": nature does nothing by "jumps," but proceeds always by gradual degrees—an assumption which will
be accepted by physicists until the advent of the quantum
theory. In any case, the argument does *not* prove that a
body moving in natural straight-line motion will continually
accelerate; all it shows (assuming the Principle of Continuity, of course) is that, *if* the body is to arrive at any particular finite non-zero velocity, it will have to pass successively through all lesser velocities; it does not show that
when any given speed is reached, the body will continue to
increase (rather than maintain or decrease) its speed beyond that until it arrives at its goal. (Indeed, at this stage
it even becomes unclear as to whether Galileo considers it
proved, or merely plausible, that such a body will continually accelerate: whereas earlier he had claimed that that
conclusion "naturally follows," he now asserts merely that
"it seems much more reasonable" to suppose that acceleration will occur.)

In any event, Galileo concludes by trying to guarantee
that the motion toward a naturally assigned place will be
in a straight line:

> This acceleration of motion occurs only when the body in
> motion keeps going, and is attained only by approaching
> its goal. So wherever its natural inclination draws it, it is
> conducted there by the shortest line; namely, the straight.
> (*Two Chief World Systems*, p. 21)

Again, however, Galileo's argument is far from airtight: the body could approach its goal by any path in which the distance continually lessens—for example, in a gradually decreasing spiral. To the argument that the path of a body moving to a natural place will be one in which the distance to the goal continually decreases, something more must be added in order to establish that that path will be one in which the distance decreases in the maximum possible way, that is, that it is a straight line.

In this part of the book Galileo offers yet a further argument, this time specifically concerning *falling* bodies, to the effect that such a body passes through every one of the infinite gradations of slowness to its terminal velocity (pp. 23–28). The argument is important because it rests on considerations about inclined planes; but the argument rests on what Galileo takes as unquestioned assumptions of a deductive argument, rather than on empirical considerations about motion along such planes. The heart of his argument is that

one cannot doubt the possibility of planes so little elevated above the horizontal *AB* that the ball may take any

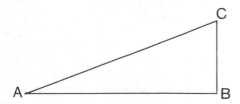

amount of time to reach the point *A*. If it is moved along the plane *BA*, an infinite time would not suffice, and the motion is retarded according as the slope is diminished. . . . Now the body falling along the perpendicular may leave from a point so near to *B* that the degree of velocity acquired at *B* would not be enough (if kept always constant) to conduct the body through a distance double the length of the inclined plane in a year, nor in ten, nor in a hundred.

We may therefore suppose it to be true that in the ordinary course of nature a body with all external and accidental impediments removed travels along an inclined plane with greater and greater slowness according as the inclination is less, until finally the slowness comes to be infinite when the inclination ends by coincidence with the horizontal plane. We may likewise suppose that the degree of velocity acquired at a given point of the inclined plane is equal to the velocity of the body falling along the perpendicular to its point of intersection with a parallel to the horizon through the given point of the inclined plane. And if these two propositions be true, it follows necessarily that a falling body starting from rest passes through all the infinite gradations of slowness . . . (*Two Chief World Systems*, pp. 27–28)

Notice particularly the appeal to the Principle of Continuity in this argument.

The remainder of this passage not only brings out Galileo's aim in the argument, but is also of crucial importance in assessing the claim that he held the principle of inertia in its modern form:

. . . and that consequently in order to acquire a determinate degree of velocity it must first move in a straight line, descending by a short or long distance according as the velocity to be acquired is to be lesser or greater, and according as the plane upon which it descends is slightly or greatly inclined. . . . In the horizontal plane no velocity whatever would ever be naturally acquired, since the body in this position would never move. But *motion in a horizontal line which is tilted neither up nor down is circular motion about the center*; therefore circular motion is never acquired naturally without straight motion to precede it; but, being once acquired, it will continue perpetually with uniform velocity. (*Two Chief World Systems*, p. 28; italics mine)

At the end of its fall (whether perpendicularly or along the inclined plane), the body will have acquired a certain terminal velocity; it will now proceed along the "horizontal"—

that is, *along a great circle of the earth's surface* (considered, in accordance with the supposition that all "external impediments" have been removed, perfectly smooth); there (by proposition 2, above) it will continue to move with uniform velocity forever. Contrary to Ernst Mach, the continuation of the body in motion along the "horizontal plane" at uniform velocity forever is not a statement (even a restricted one) of the modern law of *rectilinear* inertia; the word "horizontal," all too easily taken as meaning "straight," means rather, as Galileo explicitly states, along the spherical surface of the earth. Indeed, a few pages earlier, in giving his assent to the supposition that the impetus of a ball falling from *C* to *B* will be equal to that acquired by one falling from *C* to *A*, Sagredo already implied as much in saying that "they have both advanced equally toward the center [of the earth]" (*Two Chief World Systems*, p. 23); that is, if *O* is the center of the earth, *OA=OB*, which are thus radii of the earth, and *AB* is really an arc of the circle of the earth's surface, drawn misleadingly, because of its shortness, as a straight line. We shall return to this important point later, when we make our final assessment of the role of "inertia" in Galileo's thought.

The argument is specifically directed toward showing that the acceleration of a falling body can be used as a means of achieving a velocity which will, when the body's motion is converted into a circular path, be preserved through the "indifference" resulting from the body's being always equidistant from the center. But more generally, the argument is intended to show that *any* naturally but noncircularly moving bodies (falling or otherwise) can be used as a means of arriving at a velocity which, if the body is then diverted into a circular path, will thenceforth be preserved uniformly and perpetually, by proposition 2. The crucial factor in this *general* argument is not the equidistance of the body from the earth's center, but rather the perpetually uniform speed which is a characteristic of natural circular motion.

The argument thus appears as an attempt to back up the "Platonic" account of the origin of order: God, in the beginning, could have used straight-line motion to give the planets the velocity which His Plan required; when, through the acceleration they would acquire because of being directed toward the place God had decreed for them, they reached that place with that velocity, God diverted them into circular orbits around the sun; the acquired velocity, and the circular paths, were then preserved forever, by what we have called proposition 2.

Nevertheless, Galileo will not really accept this "Platonic" account of the origin of order; nor will he accept the view that straight-line motion is a means used to restore an order that has been disturbed. And he warns us that "I shall return to [this point about the acquisition and perpetuity of circular motion] upon some other occasion—especially since we have explored this point not to use it as a necessary demonstration, but to illustrate a Platonic concept" (*Two Chief World Systems*, p. 29). But what he will reject will not be the uniformity and perpetuity of circular motion, nor its naturalness, but rather the proposed use of straight-line motion to establish or restore order: the "if" part of proposition 4 ("If noncircular order restoring motion does indeed exist . . . ") will be rejected; there really is no noncircular order-restoring (or, presumably, creating) motion.

Proposition 5. *Really, what appears to be natural accelerated straight-line motion is uniform and circular after all.* We have been warned early in the book that this will be argued:

> The most that ought to be conceded [to the proponents of natural straight-line motion] is that just as parts of the earth, removed from the whole (that is, from the place where they naturally rest) and, in short, reduced to a bad and disordered arrangement, return to their places naturally and spontaneously in a straight motion, so it may be inferred . . . that if the terrestrial globe were forcibly removed from the place assigned to it by nature, it would return by a straight line. This, as I said, is the most that can be granted to you, even after giving you every sort of consideration. Anyone who wants to review these matters rigorously will deny at the outset that the parts of the earth, when returning to its whole, do move in a straight line and not in a circular or mixed one. (*Two Chief World Systems*, p. 33)

But it is not until well into the Second Day that Galileo returns to the subject. Sagredo opens the discussion by asking

whether you have ever thought about what one may believe with regard to the line which is described by a heavy body falling naturally from the top of the tower to its base. (*Two Chief World Systems*, p. 162)

Salviati's response is made in terms of the view that the earth is in rotation on its axis once every twenty-four hours:

Salv. . . . if one were certain about the nature of the motion with which a heavy body descends in order to get to the center of the terrestrial globe, then by combining this with the common circular motion of the diurnal rotation, one would discover exactly what sort of a line it is that the center of gravity of the body describes as a composite of those two movements.

Sagr. As to the simple movement toward the center, depending on gravity, I think that one may believe absolutely without error that it is a straight line, exactly as it would be if the earth were immovable.

Salv. . . . experience renders it certain.

Sagr. But how does experience assure us of this if we never do see any motion except that which is composed of the two, circular and downward?

Salv. Rather, Sagredo, we never see anything but the simple downward one, since this other circular one, common to the earth, the tower, and ourselves, remains imperceptible and as if non-existent. Only that of the stone, not shared by us, remains perceptible; and of this our senses show that it is along a straight line always parallel to a tower which is built upright and perpendicular on the surface of the earth. (*Two Chief World Systems*, pp. 161–62)

As we saw earlier, this is an assumption which is absolutely necessary for meeting the Aristotelian arguments against the rotation of the earth: everything in our experience must take place *just as if the earth did not rotate.* It is thus no accident that we have already encountered it in the replies to Aristotle's arguments by the Impetus Theorists, though it has come to be called the "Principle of Galilean Relativity." Galileo expresses it as follows:

> Whatever motion comes to be attributed to the earth must necessarily remain imperceptible to us and as if nonexistent, so long as we look only at terrestrial objects; for as inhabitants of the earth, we consequently participate in the same motion. . . .

> . . . Motion, insofar as it is and acts as motion, to that extent exists relatively to things that lack it; and among things which all share equally in any motion, it does not act, and is as if it did not exist. (*Two Chief World Systems*, pp. 114, 116)

We must, however, recognize that Galileo's (and, for that matter, Oresme's) understanding of this idea is very different from that of Newtonian or Einsteinian mechanics. As stated by modern physicists, the principle of Galilean (or mechanical) relativity asserts that it is impossible for an observer in an inertial reference frame to tell by any mechanical experiment (that is, by any effects that would arise from motions or associated forces) whether he is at rest or in a state of uniform rectilinear motion, and if so, at what velocity he is "really" traveling. (As opposed to this "mechanical" principle of special relativity, the Einsteinian principle of special relativity states that it is impossible for an observer in an inertial reference frame to ascertain by *any* experiment, mechanical, electromagnetic, or whatever, whether he is at rest or in uniform rectilinear motion.) But there is no indication that Galileo believes all motion to be relative in the sense that all inertial reference frames are equivalent: on the contrary, for Galileo, even though "whatever moves, moves with respect to something motionless" (*Two Chief World Systems*, p. 116), there is something truly motionless with respect to which "true and real" motions can be determined—namely, the absolutely motionless outermost sphere. (Indeed, the special principles—the "Galilean" and Einsteinian—imply that only shared *inertial* motions will go unnoticed: accelerated motions *will* have observable effects. But Galileo seems to believe that *any* shared motions, inertial or otherwise, will be unnoticeable to their sharers, and in this sense—ignoring his view that there nevertheless is "true and real" motion—his view seems closer to the Einsteinian principle of *general* relativity than to one of the special principles.)

But even when understood in its own terms, Galileo's view that shared motions will have no effects observable by the participants involves a deep ambiguity. In the Fourth Day of the *Two Chief World Systems*, Galileo contends that the most convincing proof of the earth's motion is the existence of the tides. His claim is that the tides are to be explained as the sloshing around of waters in the ocean and sea basins due to the motion of the earth. (He explicitly and vehemently rejects attempts to explain the tides in terms of an influence of the moon—after all, that would suggest the abhorrent notion of action at a distance.) But this would appear to contradict the principle of relativity, since the waters of the oceans and seas, sharing as they do the motion of the land, should not exhibit any behavior different from that of the land. Could Galileo be suggesting implicitly that the principle of relativity applies only to bodies of like kind—so that while *earthy* bodies will manifest no differential effects of shared motions, watery bodies will respond to those motions differently (and therefore observably) from earthy ones? Such a reply to the difficulty would make Galileo's theory of the tides consistent with his principle of relativity; but, unfortunately, he has already, in the Second Day, introduced the principle of relativity as part of a barrage of refutations of arguments against the possibility of the earth's motion—including the argument that the waters (and air) would behave differently, being left behind by the rotating earth to cause giant floods (and windstorms)!

However, what is interesting here is not so much whether Galileo's views are or can be made consistent, but rather the motivation behind his views. For what he is clearly interested in is the defense of Copernicanism; and on the one hand, he finds it necessary to accept the principle of relativity in order to explain the *absence* of effects that should, according to the Aristotelian-Ptolemaic tradition, appear if the earth moved; yet on the other hand, he is happy enough to argue that there *are*, nevertheless, observable effects. His commitment to Copernicanism is strong enough to lead him to pass over questions of the consistency of his views. At the end of this chapter we shall find an even more impressive example of the hold which Copernicanism exercised over his thought.

But let us return to our main line of argument. In attempting to ascertain the true path of the falling body, Salviati continues:

> It is not enough to understand that [this downward movement] is straight. It is required to know whether it is uniform or variable . . . it would be needful to know the ratio according to which such acceleration takes place. (*Two Chief World Systems*, p. 163)

This latter problem (the solution to which has been known to Galileo since at least 1604) he claims "has not been known up to now by any philosopher or mathematician whatever" (*Two Chief World Systems*, p. 163), and he thus fails to recognize, whether consciously or through ignorance, the work of medievals like Oresme. In any case, Salviati, without giving the exact "ratio" (the proportionality of distance fallen to the square of the time of fall), proceeds to discuss the path of the falling body on the basis of general considerations about the downward motion.

> Since the motion of the falling weight is continually accelerated, the line compounded of the two movements [i.e., "the straight movement toward the center of the earth . . . and the circular motion toward the east"] must have an ever-increasing ratio of successive distances from the circumference of that circle which would have been marked out by the center of gravity of the stone had it always remained on the tower. It is also required that this departure be small at the beginning—or rather minimal, even the least possible. For leaving from rest (that is, from the privation of downward motion) and entering into motion straight down, the falling weight must pass through every degree of slowness that exists between rest and any speed of motion. . . . Supposing, then, that such

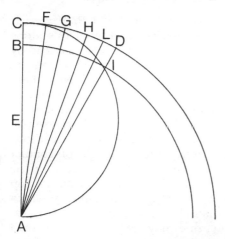

is the progress of acceleration; it being further true that the descending weight tends to end at the center of the earth, then the line of its compound motion must be such as to travel away from the top of the tower at an ever-increasing rate. To put it better, this line leaves from the circle described by the top of the tower because of the revolution of the earth, its departure from that circle being less *ad infinitum* according as the moving body is found to be less and less removed from the point where it was first placed. Moreover, this line of compound motion must tend to terminate at the center of the earth. Now, making these two assumptions, I draw the circle *BI* with *A* as a center and radius *AB*, which represents the terrestrial globe. Next, prolonging *AB* to *C*, the height of the tower *BC* is drawn; this, carried by the earth along the circumference *BI*, marks out with its top the arc *CD*.

Now dividing line *CA* at its midpoint *E*, and taking *E* as a center and *EC* as radius, the semicircle *CIA* is described along which I think it very probable that a stone dropped from the top of the tower *C* will move, with a motion composed of the general circular movement and its own straight one.

For if equal sections *CF*, *FG*, *GH*, *HL* are marked on the circumference *CD*, and straight lines are drawn to the center *A* from the points *F*, *G*, *H*, and *L*, the parts of these intercepted between the two circles *CD* and *BI* represent always the same tower *CB*, carried by the earth's globe toward *DI*. And the points where these lines are cut by the arc of the semicircle *CIA* are the places at which the falling stone will be found at the various times. Now these points become more distant from the top of the tower in an ever-increasing proportion, and that is what makes its straight motion along the side of the tower show itself to be always more and more rapid. You may also see how, thanks to the infinite acuteness of the angle of contact between the two circles *DC* and *CI*, the departure of the stone from the circumference *CFD* (that is, from the top of the tower) is very, very small at the beginning, which is the same as saying that the downward motion is extremely slow. . . . Finally, one may understand how such motion tends eventually to terminate at the center of the earth. (*Two Chief World Systems*, pp. 164–66)

Salviati draws three surprising consequences from his treatment.

The first is that if we consider the matter carefully, the body really moves in nothing other than a simple circular motion, just as when it rested on the tower it moved with a simple circular motion.

The second [is that] . . . it moves not one whit more nor less than if it had continued resting on the tower; for the arcs *CF*, *FG*, *GH*, etc., which it would have passed through staying always on the tower, are precisely equal to the arcs of the circumference *CI* corresponding to the same *CF*, *FG*, *GH*, etc. [Galileo gives the proof of this equality half a page later in the text.]

From this there follows a third marvel—that the true and real motion [*sic*] of the stone is never accelerated at all, but is always equable and uniform. For all these arcs marked equally on the circumference *CD*, and corresponding arcs marked on the circumference *CI*, are passed over in equal times. So we need not look for any other causes of acceleration or any other motions, for the moving body, whether remaining on the tower or falling, moves always in the same manner; that is, circularly, with the same rapidity, and with the same uniformity. (*Two Chief World Systems*, p. 166)

Beautiful! The bifurcation of natural motions into celestial (circular, uniform) and sublunar (rectilinear, accelerated), and of the latter into "toward the center" and "away from the center," disappears; *all* natural motion is circular, and, furthermore, as befits the natural, is uniform and eternal; and finally, its total quantity never changes: when a body in natural motion changes its path to another natural motion, its speed remains the same. (Unfortunately, the uniform speed of fall of a body would seem to imply that its momentum should be equal at every point of its fall, so that its impact should be just as strong if it were caught one foot from the origin of its fall as it would be if it were caught one hundred feet further down.) No longer need we inquire —as so many traditional thinkers had, and as Galileo himself had in *On Motion* and in the arguments of proposition 4 above—as to the cause of accelerated motion. A whole network of distinctions and problems is swept away in favor of simplicity. Sagredo draws the inevitable conclusion, to which the book has been tending all along:

According to these considerations, straight motion goes entirely out the window and nature never makes any use of it at all. Even that which you granted to it at the beginning, of restoring to their places such integral, natural bodies as were separated from the whole and badly disorganized, is now taken away and assigned to circular motion.

Salv. This would necessarily follow if the terrestrial globe were proved to move circularly, which I do not claim has been done. (*Two Chief World Systems*, p. 167)

Nevertheless, in spite of this concession to the supposed objectivity of the work with respect to the two world systems, the unity and simplicity achieved must have been appealing to Galileo and his readers, and for that reason alone the assumption of Copernicanism (or at least of the rotation of the earth, if not also its revolution around the sun) would have gained immensely in credibility. In contrast to the extension of terrestrial physics to the astronomical realm which Newton was to accomplish, Galileo has made terrestrial physics a branch of astronomy, the study of circular motion. Indeed, in this argument of Galileo's, the Circle Tradition has reached its culmination—a quarter century after Kepler announced that the planetary orbits are ellipses. (We must not, however, succumb too readily to the idea that Galileo was "committed" to the Circles idea in the same way as Aristotle, say, was. For Galileo's reasons for adopting circles are by no means the same as Aristotle's, deriving, as we have seen, from his adherence to Copernicanism. And although Galileo shares Aristotle's idea of "order" as proper positional arrangement, he nevertheless uses that concept, as Aristotle did not, to *deduce* the "naturalness" of circular motion. Thus the *total* context of the Circles idea in Galileo, compounded of Copernicanism, the positional concept of order, and, as a claimed consequence, the naturalness of circular motion, is very different from the corresponding Aristotelian picture. The idea of a "common tradition" or "paradigm"[1] misleadingly suggests a greater unity and continuity than actually existed: there was continuity, but the differences, and the reasoning behind them, must also be recognized.)

There is still room for doubt, however, because the determination of the path has not rested on an exact mathematical proof, but only on general considerations about conditions which the path must satisfy. Salviati recognizes this:

> That the descent of heavy bodies does take place in exactly this way, I will not at present declare; I shall only say that if the line described by a falling body is not exactly this, it is very near to it. (*Two Chief World Systems*, p. 167)

But how are we to take this remark? When, in 1637, Galileo's argument was criticized by Fermat (after Cavalieri, who gave credit to Galileo, had announced that the path is a parabola), Galileo responded by claiming that he had never meant the argument to be taken seriously at all.

Although it was said in the *Dialogue* that the mixture of the straight motion of the falling body and the uniform motion of the diurnal motion would perhaps give rise to a semicircle that ended in the center of the earth, this was said as a jest, as is clearly manifest, since it is called a caprice and a curiosity. . . . I wish therefore to be excused especially since this poetic fiction carries with it three unexpected consequences. (Letter to Pierre Carcavy, 5 June 1637, *Opere*, vol. 17, p. 89; trans. W. R. Shea in "The World in Motion")

But that was afterward; and contrary to his claim, it is not "clearly manifest" that the argument is a "jest." When Salviati asks Sagredo to tell him "what you think of these curiosities of mine," the intent of the word "curiosities" is clearly understatement; by no stretch of the imagination could it be interpreted in a sense consistent with "jests." But if the argument was intended as a serious one, are we to take Salviati's closing hesitation as merely the expression of a vague doubt because of the lack of complete precision of the argument, or did Galileo, at this stage, definitely believe that the path is something other than circular, though "very near to it"? And if the latter, did he believe the argument would still support Copernicanism, even though the true path of a naturally falling body is not circular? This question goes beyond one of interpreting a certain stage in Galileo's career; for we shall later see him considering, or seeming to consider, the path to be a parabola—a conclusion which, as we have just noted, was announced by Galileo's disciple Buonaventura Cavalieri in 1632, the very year the *Two Chief World Systems* appeared; and, on his master's grumblings, Cavalieri was quick to acknowledge Galileo's priority in the discovery. Yet we shall again see him doubting whether his "proof," in *Two New Sciences*, that this is the path is really a proof or merely an approximation; and this in turn will lead us into deep controversies about Galileo's view of science, his modernity, and, most specifically, the role of the principle of inertia in his thought.

Galileo's attitude toward rectilinear motion is further revealed in a passage earlier in the Second Day, in which he argues that, since such motion cannot be eternal, it therefore cannot be natural:

> For straight motion, whether you will have it be upward or downward, you yourself [Simplicio, in agreement with Aristotle] make bounded by the circumference [of the lunar sphere, or at best of the outermost sphere] and the center; hence although the movable body (that is, the earth) is eternal, yet straight motion being by its nature not eternal but bounded, the earth cannot naturally partake of it. (*Two Chief World Systems*, p. 135)

Thus the straight-line motion attributed by Aristotle as natural to the four elements—upward or downward along a radius of the universe to their natural places—cannot really satisfy the basic requirements of "natural" motion. Indeed, how could it, since violent motion is presupposed if the elements are to have been moved out of their natural places?

> You must impede them, oppose them, and force them if you want them to be moved, since once they have fallen they have to be forcibly thrown up on high in order to fall again. (*Two Chief World Systems*, p. 135)

And how could what is natural presuppose the occurrence of what is violent? (Though Galileo was willing at least to consider the "Platonic" theory of the origin of the universal order, which presupposed exactly that.) Even the most conscientious Aristotelian might have raised such a question.

Thus again, as so often, we see Galileo in agreement with fundamental Aristotelian contentions but claiming to carry them out more consistently than had Aristotle himself and his followers. For Aristotle had argued (1) that whatever is eternal is natural (though Galileo interprets him as claiming that the converse, whatever is natural is eternal, is also true), and (2) that straight-line motion cannot be eternal. And Galileo's argument is that these two propositions are inconsistent, and require the rejection of straight-line motion as natural for the sublunar elements.[2]

> Hence as to maintaining that movement by a straight line suits or could suit naturally the earth or any other mov-

able body while the rest of the universe preserved its perfect order, give up this whole idea: if you will not grant the earth circular motion, exert your strength in upholding and defending its immobility. (*Two Chief World Systems*, p. 136)

Thus the view expressed by Galileo—or at least by Salviati—in the Second Day of the book adds up to this: not only *is* there no natural straight-line motion, even of the Aristotelian up-or-down variety; the idea that any body might continue in uniform rectilinear motion forever is—for Salviati as it was for Aristotle—senseless. *For Galileo to have asserted the principle of inertia would have contradicted fundamental principles which, at least in this portion of his writings, he accepted from the Aristotelian tradition.*

But this does not mean that there are not contradictions—or at least apparent ones. For later in that same Second Day, when Galileo turns to countering Aristotle's argument that, if the earth rotated, heavy objects would be thrown off, we are told that

heavy objects, whirled quickly around a fixed center, acquire an impetus to move away from that center even when they have a natural tendency to go toward it. (*Two Chief World Systems*, p. 190)

Thus, if a bottle containing water is whirled around in a circle at the end of a cord, the water will not spill out; and furthermore, this behavior is independent of the orientation of the plane of rotation.

Whether this [whirling] is parallel to the horizon, or vertical, or slanted in another way, the water will not spill out of the bottle. (*Two Chief World Systems*, p. 190)

What, then, is the character of the tendency, of the push of the acquired impetus?

If a hole is made in the bottom of the bottle, the water will be seen to spurt forth no less toward the sky than laterally or toward the ground. . . . whirling confers an impetus upon the moving body toward the circumference, if the motion is swift. (*Two Chief World Systems*, p. 190)

Judging from this way of Galileo's putting the point, the reader might conclude that the impetus is directed, not along the *tangent* to the circle of rotation, but along a *perpendicular* thereto, that is, radially outward. This would, however, be a mistake; for, after eliciting from Simplicio a declaration that "the impressed impetus . . . is undoubtedly in a straight line" (*Two Chief World Systems*, p. 191), Salviati asks, "But what straight line?" And his answer to his question is that

> the circular motion of the projector impresses an impetus upon the projectile to move, when they separate, along the straight line tangent to the circle of motion at the point of separation, and that continuing with this motion, it travels ever farther from the thrower. . . . the projectile would continue to move along that line if it were not inclined downward by its own weight. (*Two Chief World Systems*, p. 193)

Thus the body would, when released from its circular motion, continue to move in a straight line if there were no interfering tendencies. We must take care, however, to avoid the temptation, to which so many writers have succumbed,[3] of confusing Galileo's view here with a modern conception of inertia. For his view can immediately be seen to fall short of the latter in at least four respects. (1) The motion produced is a *violent* one, brought about by an imparted impetus; it is not a "natural" state, requiring no external pushing cause, like the later inertia. (If Galileo is indeed saying that the produced motion will continue *forever* in the absence of interference, he is of course contradicting his earlier adherence to the principle that whatever is not natural cannot be eternal.) (2) This impetus is said to be conveyed by circular motion; there is no hint that an impetus conveyed by any *other* means would also produce continuous motion, or even motion in a straight line. (3) There is no mention of the produced motion's continuing at *uniform* speed—though of course there is no mention of the contrary either. (4) Galileo says that the impetus is conveyed to the moving body "if the [whirling] motion is swift"; thus slow rotation, we might expect, would not convey such an impetus. However, since this remark is not further elaborated (and since it also appears to violate the Principle of Continuity), we cannot be sure how seriously Galileo intended it to be taken.

Aside from these deviations from a true inertial concept, however, we might at least expect that Galileo has finally grasped the fact that the path of a projectile must be analyzed, not (as he earlier said) as a combination of a straight-line downward tendency, due to its natural gravity, with a *circular* tendency, due to its rotation along with the earth, but rather as a combination of the former with a *straight-line* tendency due to this imparted impetus. (And that is, as we shall see presently, the way the analysis proceeds in *Two New Sciences*—and, with certain qualifications which we shall also see, it is the way it proceeds in later "Newtonian" mechanics.) Thus, in the case of an object being carried around by the earth's rotation,

> two motions come under our consideration: a motion of projection, commencing at the point of contact and following the tangent, and another of downward tendency, commencing at the projectile and going along the secant toward the center. (*Two Chief World Systems*, p. 196)

But we get no such re-analysis of the combined effect of the two tendencies. Instead, Galileo, interested as he is here in refuting the Aristotelian argument that heavy objects would be thrown off a rotating earth, lapses into a traditional approach: different tendencies to motion do not *cooperate* to produce a *resultant* motion; they *compete*, and one or the other *prevails*. Thus he sees his problem as the following:

> To have projection [off the rotating earth] occur, it is required that the impetus along the tangent prevail over the tendency along the secant. (*Two Chief World Systems*, p. 196)

And, luckily for us who are not tied down, he manages to prove that the tendency along the secant prevails, so that we are not flung off into space. In short, in his earlier analysis of the path of a body falling on a rotating earth, Galileo had an incorrect idea of the tendencies involved, but he was "modern" at least in applying the Principle of Superposition (i.e., of combination of tendencies). Now, however, in the present analysis, the situation is exactly reversed: he now has a correct idea of the tendencies involved, but he fails to apply the Principle of Superposition to determine the path of a body having the two tendencies, preferring to remain within the confines of earlier tradition in asking only which of the two tendencies prevails (completely) over the other.

Despite the contradictions in Galileo's discussions of motion in the *Two Chief World Systems*, is it still possible that, even in that work, he really adhered to the principle of inertia, and was only *saying* that he agreed with the Aristotelian tradition for the sake of refuting it? This is what Stillman Drake, translator of the *Two Chief World Systems* and one of the foremost Galilean scholars of our time, would have us believe. It is not only in the *Two New Sciences* (in passages which we will discuss shortly), Drake claims, that we find Galileo dealing with motion in an essentially modern way; "passages on projectile motion in the *Dialogue*" (referring to pp. 174–95) show that in that work also

> Galileo as a physicist treated inertial motion as rectilinear. Nevertheless, Galileo as a propagandist, when writing the *Dialogue*, stated that rectilinear motion cannot be perpetual, though circular motion may be. In the same book he ascribed some special properties almost metaphysically to circles and circular motions. (Drake, *Galileo Studies*, p. 253)

In thus defending the essential modernity of Galileo's views of motion and arguing against the view that in the *Two Chief World Systems* he remained within the "circle" tradition, Drake maintains that the passages from which the latter sorts of interpretation "derive their only support" have a "primarily strategic character" (Drake, p. 253). According to him, "The passages in question . . . should be construed in the light of the purpose for which that book was written," which was to overcome resistance, especially on the part of Aristotelian philosophers, to Copernicanism. For this polemical purpose, "in the opening section of his book he deliberately conceded (or appeared to concede) to the philosophers everything he possibly could without compromising his one objective" (Drake, p. 253).

It was far better strategy for him to ennoble the circle, using arguments extracted from Aristotle himself, and to argue that circular motion was as suitable to the earth as to the heavens, if he wanted to win over or even neutralize any philosophers. And I can see in my mind's eye some of them starting to read the *Dialogue* for no other purpose than to find and answer hostile arguments against Aristotle, and then in the first forty or fifty pages finding themselves so much at home as to wonder whether there might not be some merit in the other ideas of so sound a writer. (Drake, p. 254)

However, solid evidence for this interpretation of Galileo as "modern" when he spoke as a "physicist" rather than as a "propagandist" is rather minimal. The basic connection which Galileo tries to establish between circular motion and Copernicanism is not confined to "the opening section of the book" or even to "the first forty or fifty pages," but permeates the entire work. It is an essential element in the unification of the terrestrial and the celestial which he expressly wishes to achieve when he argues, on the one hand, that the heavens are corruptible just as is the earth, and, on the other hand, that circular motion is as fundamental in the terrestrial realm as it is in the heavens. The analysis of projectile motion in terms of a rectilinear component, on the contrary, is confined to a scant twenty-one pages (174–95); and even there, as we have seen, the rectilinear component is treated as the result of an acquired impetus, so that it is a violent, not a natural motion.

In support of his contention, Drake argues that, elsewhere in his writings, Galileo takes a much more skeptical and critical, and even ridiculing, attitude toward the fundamentality of circles than he does in the *Two Chief World Systems*. This, he contends, shows that the role assigned to circles "almost metaphysically" in the latter work is to be looked upon solely in the light of a propagandistic motive.

When I read the metaphysical praise of circles in the *Dialogue*, I do not conclude with most historians that its author was unable to break the spell of ancient traditions; rather, I strongly suspect an ulterior purpose in those passages. This suspicion is confirmed when I read his other books and his voluminous correspondence and find nowhere else any trace of metaphysics about circles. On the contrary, Galileo often scoffs at such ideas; thus in his *Assayer*, published in 1623, he expressly denied that any geometrical form is prior or superior to any other, let alone that any shape is perfect, as Aristotle had claimed for the circle. (Drake, pp. 253–54)

But let us compare what Galileo says about circles in the *Two Chief World Systems* with what he says in the *Assayer*. In the latter work, he does indeed scoff at the idea that one geometrical form is superior to any other:

> For my own part, never having read the pedigrees and patents of nobility of shapes, I do not know which of them are more and which are less noble, nor do I know their rank in perfection. I believe that in a way all shapes are ancient and noble; or, to put it better, that none of them are noble and perfect, or ignoble and imperfect, except in so far as for building walls a square shape is more perfect than the circular, and for wagon wheels the circle is more perfect than the triangle. (*Discoveries and Opinions*, p. 263)

But these words are by no means incompatible with what Galileo says in the *Two Chief World Systems*. It is not easy to tell what Drake means when he speaks of the "metaphysical" properties attributed to circles in that work (to say nothing of his calling them "almost metaphysical"). But if we look at what Galileo actually does with circular motion there, we find him trying to *deduce* circularity from more fundamental principles, rather than merely assuming the "perfection" of circular motion. He thus sees himself as going deeper, and as providing a more solid basis for taking circular motion as fundamental, than does Aristotle.

> Having very well and methodically begun his discourse, at this point—being more intent upon arriving at a goal previously established in his mind than upon going wherever his steps directly lead him—[Aristotle] cuts right across the path of his discourse and assumes it as

a known and manifest thing that the motions directly upward and downward correspond to fire and earth. Therefore it is necessary that beyond those bodies, which are close to us, there must be some other body in nature to which circular motion must be suitable. This must, in turn, be as much more excellent as circular motion is more perfect than straight. Just how much more perfect the former is than the latter, he determines from the perfection of the circular line over the straight. He calls the former perfect and the latter imperfect; imperfect, because if it is infinite, it lacks an end and termination, while if finite, there is something outside of it in which it might be prolonged. This is the cornerstone, basis, and foundation of the entire structure of the Aristotelian universe, upon which are superimposed all other celestial properties—freedom from gravity and levity, ingenerability, incorruptibility, exemption from all mutations except local ones, etc. All these properties he attributes to a simple body with circular motion. The contrary qualities of gravity or levity, corruptibility, etc., he assigns to bodies naturally movable in a straight line.

Now whenever defects are seen in the foundations, it is reasonable to doubt everything else that is built upon them. I do not deny that what Aristotle has introduced up to this point, with a general discourse upon universal first principles, is reinforced with specific reasons and experiments later on in his argument, all of which must be separately considered and weighed. But what has already been said does present many and grave difficulties, whereas basic principles and fundamentals must be secure, firm, and well established, so that one may build confidently upon them. Hence before we multiply doubts, *it would not be amiss to see whether (as I believe) we may, by taking another path, discover a more direct and certain road, and establish our basic principles with sounder architectural precepts.* (*Two Chief World Systems*, pp. 18–19; italics mine)

Thus Aristotle's error lay in merely assuming, on inadequate grounds at best, the "perfection" of circular motion; and what Galileo had done so mercilessly in the *Assayer* was to point out some of the "many and grave difficulties" in that gratuitous assumption. But here Galileo, beginning with deeper principles with which everyone, including himself, could agree, avoids making such gratuitous (metaphysical?) assumptions by arguing that natural circular motion is a logical consequence of the basic assumption of an ordered universe. By this argument he tries to "establish our basic principles with sounder architectural precepts."

On other occasions when Galileo agrees with an Aristotelian doctrine, no matter how central it is, merely for the sake of argument, he says so, as in the case of the finitude of the universe:

> I might very reasonably dispute whether there is in nature such a center [of the universe], seeing that neither you nor anyone else has so far proved whether the universe is finite and has a shape, or whether it is infinite and unbounded. Still, conceding to you for the moment that it is finite and of bounded spherical shape, and therefore has its center, it remains to be seen how credible it is that the earth rather than some other body is to be found at that center. (*Two Chief World Systems*, pp. 319–20)

(Yet even here, where he specifically questions the proposition being assumed, it is far from certain that Galileo actually believed the opposite of the Aristotelian doctrine whose foundation he was questioning.) Granted, this passage occurs late in the book, and one could still argue that when Aristotelian premises were introduced at the beginning of the book, Galileo, for propagandistic reasons, might not have let us know that he was agreeing with them only for the sake of argument. We even have an example: when Simplicio exclaims, at the beginning of the book, "Think how much faster a chunk of pure earth drops than does a stick of wood!" (*Two Chief World Systems*, p. 17), the remark is let pass, as though tacitly admitted by all. Criticism does, of course, come later. Why, then, if Galileo was not really in agreement about the fundamentality of circular motion, did he not likewise question that assumption later, when the Aristotelian philosophers had presumably been softened up for the blow? We would especially expect him to do so if the opposing, rectilinear, view was indeed basic to his thought "as a physicist." As Drake himself notes, Galileo was not a man to conceal his opinions; surely, on so important a point, he would not have hidden his beliefs. Indeed, Drake warns us against assuming hidden beliefs on Galileo's part: "I see little point in looking for hidden beliefs behind the words of a man who spent his last years under arrest for disdaining to conceal his convictions" (Drake, *Galileo Studies*, p. 254). Yet is this not precisely what Drake is asking us to look for when he claims that Galileo was talking in terms of a view which was not really his own throughout much of the *Two Chief World Systems?*

We come finally, then, to the view of inertial motion expressed by Galileo in his *Two New Sciences*, at the beginning of the Fourth Day. Here we are asked to

> imagine any particle projected along a horizontal plane without friction; then we know . . . that this particle will move along this same plane with a motion which is uniform and perpetual, provided the plane has no limits. But if the plane is limited and elevated, then the moving particle, which we imagine to be a heavy one, will on passing over the edge of the plane acquire, in addition to its previous uniform and perpetual motion, a downward propensity due to its own weight; so that the resulting motion which I call projection, is compounded of one which is uniform and horizontal and of another which is vertical and naturally accelerated. (*Two New Sciences*, p. 234)

On this basis, Galileo is able to establish

> THEOREM I, PROPOSITION I. A projectile which is carried by a uniform horizontal motion compounded with a naturally accelerated vertical motion describes a path which is a semi-parabola. (*Two New Sciences*, p. 235)

Here at last, the treatment of the motion of a projectile is clearly given in terms of a composition of two straight-line tendencies: a uniform horizontal one and a vertical accelerated one. Furthermore, the deduction is made rigorously on the correct assumption that the acceleration is proportional to the square of the time; the resulting path is (a segment of) a parabola. (Sagredo points to a further assumption of the argument: "that such motions and velocities as these combine without altering, disturbing, or hindering each other, so that as the motion proceeds the path of the projectile does not change into a different curve" (*Two New Sciences*, p. 240).) Surely with this we have finally arrived at modern physics!

Again, though, the situation is not so clear-cut; Simplicio raises the kind of objection with which we are already familiar from our discussion of the *Two Chief World Systems*.

> We suppose the horizontal plane, which slopes neither up nor down, to be represented by a straight line as if each point on this line were equally distant from the center, which is not the case; for as one starts from the middle [of the line] and goes toward either end, he departs farther and farther from the center [of the earth] and is therefore constantly going uphill. (*Two New Sciences*, p. 240)

The perpetual continuation of motion is, once more, not along a straight line, but along a great circle around the center of the earth; and this circular path is *not* viewed as a deviation from a tangential tendency due to gravitation. Salviati, speaking for "our Author," Galileo, grants the objection, admitting that the straight-line treatment is only an approximation, but one which is allowable given the shortness of the horizontal component in comparison with the size of the earth.

> All these difficulties and objections which you urge are so well founded that it is impossible to remove them; and, as for me, I am ready to admit them all, which indeed I think our Author would also do. I grant that these conclusions proved in the abstract will be different when applied in the concrete and will be fallacious to this extent, that neither will the horizontal motion be uniform nor the natural acceleration be in the ratio assumed, nor the path of the projectile a parabola, etc. But, on the other hand, I ask you not to begrudge our Author that which other eminent men have assumed even if not strictly true.

The authority of Archimedes alone will satisfy everybody. In his Mechanics and in his first quadrature of the parabola he takes for granted that the beam of a balance or steelyard is a straight line, every point of which is equidistant from the common center of all heavy bodies, and that the cords by which heavy bodies are suspended are parallel to each other.

Some consider this assumption permissible because, in practice, our instruments and the distances involved are so small in comparison with the enormous distance from the center of the earth that we may consider a minute of arc on a great circle as a straight line, and may regard the perpendiculars let fall from its two extremities as parallel. (*Two New Sciences*, pp. 240–41)

So again, as in the *Two Chief World Systems*, the conclusion here in *Two New Sciences* is admitted as being only approximately true: the situation has not been treated with complete precision, but has been *falsified* in certain respects in order to simplify calculations. A truly accurate calculation (for the case of motion in a void, i.e., with no extraneous agencies at work) would be based on a combination of a downward, accelerated, rectilinear motion with a "horizontal," uniform, circular component.

In the light of Galileo's commitment to Copernicanism, we can understand and perhaps even appreciate his attitude toward this argument. In 1610 and thereafter he had obtained unassailable evidence for Copernicanism. We have seen how, in subsequent years, and culminating in the arguments of the *Two Chief World Systems*, he had come to couple that doctrine, and its defense, with a view that circular motion was "natural" to the earth as well as to the heavens, and, furthermore, with a view that the very concept of an ordered universe implied that circular motion and only circular motion was "natural." The *Two Chief World Systems* was an attempt to carry out those views. Yet before 1610, independently of Copernicanism, Galileo had arrived at certain views concerning motion, to which now, after 1630, he returned in earnest. On the basis of those ideas and a geometrical construction, he now found that the path of a projectile was a parabola. But against the background of the ideas which he had been developing and to which he had been increasingly committed, even in the face of personal tragedy, since 1610, this deduction *could* not be accepted as correct, at least as it stood: if Copernicanism was to be retained, that proof *had* to be viewed as only "approximate." The key to doing so, of course, lay in viewing the horizontal component in the geometrical construction as an approximation to a true circular path. Thus, behind the scenes of its concern with mechanics, the *Two New Sciences* is still Copernican in spirit if not in word; and it is that very Copernicanism, ultimately, that led Galileo to view the parabolic trajectory, and therefore the rectilinearity of the horizontal component, as mere idealizations.

Yet, as so many times in the history of science, Galileo's treatment, which he himself considered as an idealization, came to be accepted by his successors as a literally correct treatment: the *true* horizontal component *was* a straight line, and deviation therefrom was due to the action of an external force, gravity. Just so, Max Planck in 1900 considered his introduction of discrete (quantum) considerations into the analysis of black-body radiation to be a mere calculational device, not corresponding to anything in reality, which—as was demonstrated by all the successful theories of classical physics—had to exhibit continuity in such processes. It was Einstein who, in 1905, first proposed that the quantum be taken seriously; Planck himself did not believe in the *truth* of the step in his argument that relied on quantum considerations.[4] But (a) the power and generality of Planck's calculations (which not only were precise but also yielded a single general formula to cover all black-body radiation frequencies); (b) the successful applications of quantum considerations to other areas, beginning with Einstein's work on the photoelectric effect; and (c) ultimately, the possibility of *explaining* the "continuity" postulated by classical theories in terms of a deeper discreteness—all led science ultimately to accept Einstein's approach rather than Planck's; to believe, that is, in the correctness, rather than in the mere convenience, of the quantum approach.

Some claim that Galileo and Planck were so "absorbed" or "dominated" by traditional ideas that they were psychologically unable to take the step to a new idea to which their own work pointed. Whether this psychological analysis is correct or not, there certainly was abundant *reason* for them to remain faithful to traditional principles, and to consider their approach as a mere calculational device: for the principle of circularity in pre-Galilean physics, like the principle of continuity in pre-Planckian physics, had played a fundamental role in theories that had been generally successful over a wide range of experience. In addition, Galileo had two further reasons for continuing to adhere to the traditional principle: first, he had (or believed he had) provided a deeper justification for the principle than had been offered by earlier adherents of it, namely by deducing it from the more fundamental principle of the orderliness of nature; and second, he had (or thought he had) integrated that traditional postulate of circularity with a modern idea, Copernicanism, into what he took to be a successful synthesis.

Planck himself was able to formulate the quantum principle (at least in a restricted form relevant to the case with which he dealt, black-body radiation); Galileo never gave an explicit and full statement of the principle of inertia. He was, it is true, occasionally on the brink of having the principle, both in the *Two Chief World Systems* (pages 174–95) and in his application of it to the case of projectile paths in *Two New Sciences*. But we must not allow these passages to obscure other facts: in most passages in *Two Chief World Systems*, and in his analysis of his own argument about the path of projectiles in *Two New Sciences*, he definitely shied away from the modern principle. On the other hand, the fact that he, like Planck, failed to go all the way in the direction of subsequent thought must not detract from their contributions: for it was they who made the important move away from the traditional idea, even though it was left to others to carry out a full expression of those ideas, and to consider those ideas to be representative of nature rather than mere calculational devices.

In assessing the degree to which Galileo approached the principle of inertia in its modern form, it is necessary to examine carefully the question of what "full possession" of that principle would involve—that is, the question of what the various conceptual components of that principle are. The following are perhaps the most important of these:

1. The motion of the body in question is *uncaused* (or "natural"); that is, it takes place without a pushing agency, external or internal.
2. The motion of the body *continues perpetually*, unless it is interfered with by an extrinsic agency.
3. The motion is *rectilinear*.
4. The speed is *uniform* (so long as the body moves).
5. The motion has *no preferential direction* (that is, there is no "inclination" or "repugnance" to motion in any particular direction, like "up" or "down"; natural motion can take place in any direction).
6. *Rest is on a par* with inertial motion, in the sense that a body once in either such state will remain in that state unless acted upon by an extrinsic agency.

Note that the truth of each of these six conditions is independent of that of the others. For example, the universe might have been so constructed that the first was true but the second false, bodies "naturally" coming to a stop (whether by decelerating or stopping suddenly after a period of uniform motion). The first and second could be true while the third was false; and so on. On the other hand, although these are the most important features of the principle of inertia, the list is not exhaustive: specific propositions of specific theories might contradict the principle in ways not covered by this or any finite list. For example, Moody emphasizes that a precondition for arriving at the principle of inertia was to overcome the arguments against the possibility of motion at a finite speed in a vacuum. This is why he emphasizes the role of Avempace's formula, $V = F - R$. (On the other hand, Descartes, who denied the possibility of a void, at least stated the principle, whether consistently or not. Note, incidentally, that Moody's principle, together with principles 1 and 3, are essentially the steps outlined in the third section of chapter 2, above, as necessary if the transition from impetus to inertial physics were to have been made.) Again, although Descartes is usually given credit for having presented the first clear formulation of the principle of inertia, in 1644—and he certainly did formulate it—nevertheless, in the general context of his scientific-philosophical system, the principle is not merely false, but unintelligible. For in that system, which identifies matter and space, it is utter nonsense to suppose that one body might be isolated from the influence of other bodies (i.e., that a volume of space be isolated from the adjoining space).

But in terms of these six components, we can review some of the arguments concerning Galileo's "possession" of the principle of inertia.

Stillman Drake's view is that Galileo did have the "essential core" of the principle of inertia.

> In my opinion the essential core of the inertial concept lies in the ideas . . . of a body's indifference to motion or to rest and its continuance in the state it is once given. This idea is, to the best of my knowledge, original with Galileo. It is not derived from, or even compatible with, impetus theory, which assumed a natural tendency of every body to come to rest. (Drake, *Galileo Studies*, p. 251)

Drake finds the root of these ideas in a distinction made by Galileo as early as *On Motion* (chap. 16, pp. 72 ff.) between natural motion, violent motion, and a third type not recognized by Aristotle, neutral motion. The latter arises when a body is moving but maintaining the same distance from the center of the earth, so that it has no natural inclination in an upward or downward direction. It also arises in the case of any rotating homogeneous sphere, no matter where located, "since for every part of that sphere which was approaching the center of the earth at a given moment, an equal part would be receding from it; thus the sphere as a whole would be moving, but neither naturally nor violently" (Drake, *Galileo Studies*, p. 249). By the first decade of the seventeenth century, Galileo had taken a further step, as indicated in a letter of 1607 from a former pupil, Castelli, referring to Galileo's doctrine "that although to start motion a mover is necessary, yet to continue it the absence of opposition is sufficient" (quoted in Drake, *Galileo Studies*, p. 250). The full statement of Galileo's view is found by Drake in a passage in the *Letters on Sunspots* (1613):

> I have observed that physical bodies have an inclination toward some motion, as heavy bodies downward, which motion is exercised by them through an intrinsic property and without need of a special external mover, whenever they are not impeded by some obstacle. And to some other motion they have a repugnance, as the same heavy bodies to motion upward, wherefore they never move in that manner unless thrown violently upward by an external mover. Finally, to some movements they are indifferent, as are heavy bodies to horizontal motion, to which they have neither inclination . . . nor repugnance. And therefore, all external impediments removed, a heavy body on a spherical surface concentric with the earth will be indifferent to rest or movement toward any part of the horizon. And it will remain in that state in which it has once been placed; that is, if placed in a state of rest, it will conserve that; and if placed in movement toward the west, for example, it will maintain itself in that movement. Thus a ship . . . having once received some impetus through the tranquil sea, would move continually around our globe without ever stopping . . . if . . . all external impediments could be removed. (*Discoveries and Opinions*, pp. 113–14)

It must be noted first that this passage is perfectly compatible with a conserved impetus theory of the Buridan sort, with the impetus being a circular one. (Drake's allegation that the "impetus theory . . . assumed a natural tendency of every body to come to rest" is true only for the self-consuming and *inclinatio ad quietem* versions of that theory.) And if it is so interpreted, Galileo's view fails to satisfy component 1 on our list: the motion is caused by an extrinsically applied impetus, which happens to be conserved. But even apart from this, it fails to satisfy at least one other condition, namely 3, that the motion be rectilinear. (It is perhaps debatable whether it also fails to satisfy 5, that the motion have no preferential direction.) Now the way in which Drake argues is interesting: he holds that the conditions which *are* satisfied by Galileo's conception are the "essential core" of the inertial concept. And hence we must conclude that rectilinearity is not part of that "essential core." But surely we must ask how Drake decides what is and what is not part of the "essence" of the principle of inertia; surely the role of rectilinearity was a highly important feature of the contrast between modern and medieval physics; it played, for example, a very concrete role in the calculation of the path of a projectile, as we have seen. Other historians, indeed, have taken a view opposite to that of Drake, holding that, because Galileo did not have the idea of rectilinear inertia, he therefore did not "possess" the modern concept of inertia *at all*. This suggestion, then, is that, contrary to Drake, rectilinearity *is* "essential" to the modern concept. This is the way Koyré seems to have argued: that Galileo's "circular inertia" was not the modern concept because it was concerned with circular motion.[5] And this is precisely the way Drake sees the contrast between his interpretation and Koyré's: "for [Koyré], the limitation of the inertial concept to uniform rectilinear motions was every bit as important as the recognition of continuance in a state of rest or motion by a body otherwise undisturbed" (Drake, *Galileo Studies*, p. 247). Drake's opinion, on the other hand, "is that the essential aspect of the concept of inertia is that of motion and rest as states of a body which are indifferently conserved" (Drake, *Galileo Studies*, p. 247). Drake and Koyré are thus *in agreement* that Galileo did not have the rectilinearity idea; their debate is *only* over whether this implies that Galileo did or did not have the "essential core" of the modern concept. The facts remain the same whichever way they are characterized: Galileo had some aspects of the modern concept and did not have others. How ironic it is that historians of science should obscure those facts by remaining hypnotized by the ancient Aristotelian idea of "essences," which is so inappropriate and misleading when applied to questions about the development of ideas![6]

5

Reason and Experience in Galileo's Thought

There are abundant references in Galileo's major works, the *Two Chief World Systems* and the *Two New Sciences*, to experiments performed and observations made; and there are also abundant references indicating that Galileo believed he *ought* to rely on observation and experiment either as the source or the confirmation of his ideas. "Our discourses," he tells us, "must relate to the sensible world and not to one on paper" (*Two Chief World Systems*, p. 113); he declares that "what sensible experience shows ought to be preferred over any argument, even one that seems to be extremely well-founded"; and he proposes that "in order not to proceed arbitrarily or at random, but with a rigorous method, let us first seek to make sure by experiments repeated many times how much time is taken by a ball of iron, say, to fall to earth from a height of one hundred yards" (*Two Chief World Systems*, p. 223).

Yet there are also many references which appear to deny the importance of observation and experiment. On one occasion, Salviati declares that "without experiment, I am sure that the effect will happen as I tell you, because it must happen that way" (*Two Chief World Systems*, p. 145). And in a famous passage, we read:

Nor can I ever sufficiently admire the outstanding acumen of those who have taken hold of this [Pythagorean, i.e., Copernican] opinion and accepted it as true; they have through sheer force of intellect done such violence to their own senses as to prefer what reason told them over that which sensible experience plainly showed them to the contrary. For the arguments against the whirling of the earth which we have already examined are very plausible, as we have seen; and the fact that the Ptolemaics and Aristotelians and all their disciples took them to be conclusive is indeed a strong argument of their effectiveness. But the experiences which overtly contradict the annual movement are indeed so much greater in their apparent force that, I repeat, there is no limit to my astonishment when I reflect that Aristarchus and Copernicus were able to make reason so conquer sense that, in defiance of the latter, the former became mistress of their belief. (*Two Chief World Systems*, p. 328)

No wonder that Simplicio complains that "in the Copernican doctrine the senses must be denied" (*Two Chief World Systems*, p. 253), and more generally that Salviati wishes "to deny not only the principles of the sciences, but palpable experience and the very senses themselves" (*Two Chief World Systems*, p. 34). Indeed, again and again in that work, it is Simplicio, not Salviati, who defends the role of the senses in the acquisition of knowledge, and calls for experiments. Then, too, it has been pointed out by many historians of science that many of Galileo's alleged "experiments" seem unlikely ever to have been performed, and are to be understood more as "thought experiments" than as actual ones. Salviati often speaks in this fashion: for example, he says that "if you want to present a more suitable experiment, you ought to say what would be observed (if not with one's actual eyes, at least with those of the mind)"; to which Simplicio replies, characteristically, "It would be necessary to be able to make such an experiment and then to decide according to the result" (*Two Chief World Systems*, p. 143). And as to still other experiments that he does seem to have performed, they are often described in such a cavalier manner that some interpreters have concluded that Galileo did not put much stock in them, intending them as mere rough illustrations of what he was already convinced of by reason.

The implications are deep: the empiricist interpretation of Galileo's work, and of science generally, is downgraded or rejected; and an alternative picture of scientific innovation comes to the fore. Such a picture has been advocated and developed in detail through the immense scholarship of Alexandre Koyré and his followers. For Koyré, as for others, the main problem of the historian with regard to Galileo and the scientific revolution is the following:

> We have to . . . explain why *modern* physics was able to adopt this principle [of inertia]; to understand why, and how, the principle of inertial motion, which to us appears so simple, so clear, so plausible and even self-evident, acquired this status of self-evidence and *a priori* truth whereas for the Greeks as well as for the thinkers of the Middle Ages the idea that a body once put in motion will continue to move forever, appeared as obviously and evidently false, and even absurd. (Koyré, "Galileo and Plato," in Wiener and Noland, *Roots of Scientific Thought*, p. 150)

Koyré finds that the transition was not at all brought about by careful observation and experiment: "observation and experience, in the sense of brute, common-sense experience, did not play a major role—or, if it did, it was a negative one, the role of obstacle—in the foundation of modern science" (Wiener and Noland, p. 149). On the contrary,

> what the founders of modern science, among them Galileo, had to do, was not to criticize and to combat certain faulty theories, and to correct or to replace them by better ones. They had to do something quite different. They had to destroy one world and to replace it by another. They had to reshape the framework of our intellect itself, to restate and reform its concepts, to evolve a new approach to Being, a new concept of knowledge, a new concept of science—and even to replace a pretty natural approach, that of common sense, by another which is not natural at all. (Wiener and Noland, p. 152)

What is this new concept of knowledge, of science? According to Koyré,

> it is the right of mathematical science, of the mathematical explanation of Nature, in opposition to the non-mathematical one of common sense and of Aristotelian physics, much more than the opposition between two astronomical

systems, that forms the real subject of the *Dialogue on the Two Greatest Systems of the World.* . . . the solution of the astronomical problem depends on the constitution of a new Physics; which in turn implies the solution of the *philosophical* question of the role played by mathematics in the constitution of the science of Nature. (Wiener and Noland, p. 166)

Thus a fundamental shift of philosophical viewpoint, rather than the refutation by experiment and observation of an old theory and its replacement by a new one, constituted the scientific revolution. It was not experiment or observation, but reason, which played the key role in the transition from medieval to modern physics; and the crucial question was that of the role of mathematics in understanding nature. But, Koyré alleges,

the 'question' about the role and the nature of mathematics constitutes the principal subject of opposition between Aristotle and Plato. . . . If you claim for mathematics a superior status, if more than that you attribute to it a real value and a commanding position in Physics, you are a Platonist. If on the contrary you see in mathematics an abstract science, which is therefore of a lesser value than those—physics and metaphysics—which deal with real being; if in particular you pretend that physics needs no other basis than experience and must be built directly on perception, that mathematics has to content itself with the secondary and subsidiary role of a mere auxiliary, you are an Aristotelian. (Wiener and Noland, pp. 167–68)

The "Platonic" character of Galileo's thought is asserted even more explicitly and fully in another article by Koyré, "Galileo and the Scientific Revolution":

It is thought, pure unadulterated thought, and not experience or sense-perception, as until then [i.e., in the Aristotelian tradition], that gives the basis for the "new science" of Galileo Galilei. . . . [According to Galileo] good physics is made *a priori*. Theory precedes fact. Experience is useless because before any experience we are already in possession of the knowledge we are seeking for.

Fundamental laws of motion (and of rest), laws that determine the spatio-temporal behavior of material bodies, are laws of a mathematical nature. Of the same nature as those which govern relations and laws of figures and of numbers. We find and discover them not in Nature, but in ourselves, in our mind, in our memory, as Plato long ago has taught us. (Koyré, *Metaphysics and Measurement*, p. 13)

The philosophy of science attributed to Galileo is clearly Koyré's own: "I should like to claim for [Galileo] the glory and merit of having known how to dispense with experiments (shown to be nowise indispensable by the very fact of his having been able to dispense with them): yet the experiments were unrealizable in practice with the facilities at his disposal" (Koyré, *Metaphysics and Measurement*, p. 75). "It is not by following experiment, but by outstripping experiment, that the scientific mind makes progress" (Ibid., p. 80). Thus "the rise and growth of experimental science is not the source but, on the contrary, the result of the new *theoretical*, that is, the new *metaphysical* approach to nature that forms the content of the scientific revolution of the seventeenth century" (Koyré, "The Significance of the Newtonian Synthesis," in *Newtonian Studies*, p. 6). The striking reversal of Mach's view of Galileo, science, and the scientific revolution hardly needs to be pointed out.

But can this "Platonic," "rationalistic" interpretation be borne out? Let us concentrate on the case of Galileo. Certainly it is true that there are numerous indications of reverence for Plato in Galileo's works, and it may well be true that many of Galileo's contemporaries gave the appellation "Platonist" to anyone who considered mathematics a key to the understanding of nature. However, our concern is not with whether Galileo and some of his contemporaries *thought* of themselves as Platonists; rather, our interest is in whether he, and the scientific revolution, really were Platonic; that is, whether, or to what extent, they exhibited the chief tenets of Plato's own thought. For our primary question concerns the extent to which Galileo and the scientific revolution can be appropriately characterized as "empiricist" or "rationalist," or as "Platonist" in contrast to

"Aristotelian." We can therefore ask whether the fundamental doctrines of Plato's thought, as summarized in chapter 2, are found in Galileo's work.

The most immediately obvious suggestion of Platonic influence in Galileo's writings is in Salviati's constant use of the "Socratic" method of cross-examination to elicit from Simplicio truths "already known" to him, "though perhaps without [his] realizing" that he knew them (*Two Chief World Systems*, p. 12). Such references which abound throughout Galileo's two major works in dialogue form, suggest that he accepted Plato's doctrine of reminiscence or recollection. And indeed there are passages that apparently make such acceptance completely explicit; most famous of these is this one:

> If you are satisfied now, Simplicio, you can see how you yourself really knew that the earth shone no less than the moon, and that not my instruction but merely *the recollection of certain things already known to you* have made you sure of it. For I have not shown you that the moon shines more brilliantly by night than by day; you already knew it, as you also knew that a little cloud is brighter than the moon. Likewise you knew that the illumination of the earth is not seen at night, and in short you knew everything in question without being aware that you knew it. Hence there should be no reason that it should be hard for you to grant that reflection from the earth can illuminate the dark part of the moon with no less a light than that with which the moon lights up the darkness of the night. (*Two Chief World Systems*, pp. 89–90; italics mine)

On another occasion, in the face of Salviati's cross-examination, Simplicio remarks that

> I have frequently studied your manner of arguing, which gives me the impression that you lean toward Plato's opinion that *nostrum scire sit quoddam reminisci* [i.e., our knowledge is a kind of recollection]. So please remove all question for me by telling me your idea of this. (*Two Chief World Systems*, pp. 190–91)

Salviati's reply is somewhat evasive: "How I feel about Plato's opinion I can indicate to you by means of words and also by deeds." However, after having drawn the desired answer to the issue under debate out of Simplicio, he remarks, "Listen to that, Sagredo; here is the *quoddam reminisci* in action, sure enough" (*Two Chief World Systems*, p. 191)

But whether or not Galileo thought of himself as endorsing fully the Platonic doctrine of reminiscence, his actual arguments fail to show that he is in complete accord with Plato. For note, in the example concerning the illumination of the moon quoted above, that what are appealed to are previous common experiences which Simplicio had had, but which he had not adequately thought about. The "Socratic" method of cross-examination, though it is coupled with a doctrine of "recollection," is not the sole property of a Platonic philosophy according to which knowledge is not acquired through sensory experience, but is innate in the mind from birth, having been acquired by the soul through exposure to the Forms prior to birth. On the contrary, the Socratic method of questioning is perfectly compatible with a theory of knowledge according to which the "recollection" involved is of knowledge originally acquired through the senses. In that case, the method is used to get the person to remember and think about his own prior sensory experience. And further, this theory of knowledge is also compatible with the view, maintained by Aristotle, that experience can be a source of absolutely certain (necessary) truth. Thus the fact that Galileo often speaks of scientific truth as necessary or certain cannot serve as evidence against his believing (or at least practicing the view) that sensory experience is the source of knowledge. Therefore, despite his constant appeal to recollection, and his often-stated (though sometimes contradicted) view that scientific truth is necessary truth, there is no evidence that Galileo accepted the doctrine of Forms in its Platonic sense.

But even if Galileo *had believed* that scientific truths (or at least basic ones) are ultimately "rational" rather than "empirical" in origin, and that he himself had arrived at his conclusions by "reason" rather than by "experience," the question would still remain as to whether he actually *could* have arrived at them in this way. For the view that there are some propositions which, while true of the world of sense-experience, are nevertheless arrived at wholly indedendently of any such experience whatever (e.g., by "reason"), is at least highly questionable. By reasoning, we are certainly able to *deduce* conclusions *given* appropriate *premises*, which, if true, must lead to true conclusions. But the history of science and philosophy has not dealt kindly with the further view that, in addition to this deductive capacity, Reason is also able, without reliance on any sensory experience at all, to *discover* truths which can then serve as premises for its deductive capacity. And if Reason has no such capacity for discovery, then any belief Galileo might have had (if indeed he did) that scientific truth is or ought to be discovered by reason rather than by observation of nature *could* not have been in accord with his actual practice. There are, as we have seen, abundant grounds for questioning Koyré's view that Galileo *was* a "rationalist," in the Platonic (or any other) sense; but even if he had been, we would still have to be skeptical as to Koyré's further view, that that belief was or could have been relevant (except possibly as a hindrance) to the processes by which he actually arrived at his scientific conclusions. And we would have to be still more skeptical about Koyré's more general view that, at critical junctures in its history, science does and ought to proceed "rationally" as opposed to "empirically."

The possibility still remains, of course, that Galileo might have *thought* of himself as having deduced at least some truths from premises discovered by reason; and we shall have to examine this possibility, and its relation to the question of "Platonism," later.

But what of other important facets of the Platonic philosophy? In assessing Galileo's attitude toward science, and the attitude of post-Galilean (but pre–twentieth-century) science in general, we will find the relation of those attitudes toward the Platonic doctrine of the Receptacle to be of the most profound significance.

The Platonic Receptacle, it will be remembered, was a principle of resistance to form, to determinateness. No form could be completely or perfectly realized in the realm of Becoming, of physical nature. Nature—the world in which we live, the world of change, of Becoming—contains an essentially irrational element: nothing in it can be described *exactly* by reason, and in particular by mathematical concepts and laws; and any deviations from those concepts or laws are inherently unexplainable. For Plato, *there is an inherent indeterminacy in nature which makes a precise description of it or anything in it impossible in principle.*

In regard to this view, early modern science (and indeed classical, i.e., prequantum science in general) was profoundly anti-Platonic: it rejected the characteristically Platonic view that nature cannot be explained completely by scientific or mathematical laws. For the science of the seventeenth century, every deviation from the behavior specified by a scientific law can in principle be explained in terms of counterforces which themselves obey precise laws.[1] Thus, for example, the failure of bodies to act according to the law of inertia is not due to any inherent stubbornness or vagueness or irrationality of nature: counterforces like friction or air resistance, themselves describable (at least "in principle") in precise mathematical detail, are responsible. There is nothing about *nature* that precludes the construction of a completely detailed and precise science; if that cannot be done, it is only because of the limitations of *our* abilities (and this explains the qualifying phrase "in principle" employed in the preceding sentences). The culminating statement of this viewpoint is found in the work of Pierre Simon de Laplace at the end of the eighteenth century:

> Given for one instant an intelligence which could comprehend all the forces by which nature is animated and the respective situation of the beings who compose it—an intelligence sufficiently vast to submit these data to analysis—it would embrace in the same formula the movements

of the greatest bodies of the universe and those of the lightest atom; for it, nothing would be uncertain and the future, as the past, would be present to its eyes. (Laplace, *A Philosophical Essay on Probabilities*, p. 4)

Finite man, on the other hand, beset with ignorance and inability to cope with the complexities of nature, must be content with probabilities rather than certainties.

The contrast between the Platonic and the classical scientific viewpoint can be seen most sharply in their respective attitudes toward the relation of mathematics to the interpretation of nature. According to the *Timaeus*, the Demiurge "began by giving [each of the four elements] a distinct configuration by means of shapes and numbers," and, in doing so, "framed them with the greatest possible perfection, which they had not before" (*Timaeus*, 53B). And as to "their numbers, their motions, and their powers," he "adjusted them in due proportion, when he had brought them in every detail to the most exact perfection permitted by Necessity [i.e., by the Receptacle]" (Ibid., 56C).[2] Shape and number are the fundamental distinguishing characteristics of the elements, and this fact explains why geometry is the key to grasping the physical. But those geometrical characteristics are imposed only "to the most exact perfection permitted" by the Receptacle; thus a geometrical treatment of bodies, for Plato, will be and can be no more than a rough treatment: their shapes are and can be only imperfect embodiments of the ideal shapes in terms of which they are described, these latter belonging to the eternal, unchangeable, intelligible realm of mathematical Forms. Mathematics is necessary for the treatment of bodies, because the elemental bodies are constructed as geometrical entities; but still the treatment cannot be exact, because those geometrical patterns are not fulfilled perfectly in the physical world.

Galileo certainly has in common with Plato the view that geometry is the key to the understanding of nature:

Philosophy is written in this grand book, the universe, which stands continually open to our gaze. But the book cannot be understood unless one first learns to comprehend the language and read the letters in which it is composed. It is written in the language of mathematics, and its characters are triangles, circles, and other geometric figures without which it is humanly impossible to understand a single word of it. (*The Assayer,* in Drake, *Discoveries and Opinions of Galileo*, pp. 237–38)[3]

But the question remains as to whether Galileo took that language as capable (at least "in principle," i.e., if our intelligence were great enough) of giving a complete account of nature, or whether it was limited by an inherent unintelligibility of nature. In favor of the former view, we have an interesting exchange in *Two Chief World Systems.* Upon Sagredo's reiteration of the view that "it must be admitted that trying to deal with physical problems without geometry is attempting the impossible" (*Two Chief World Systems*, p. 203), Simplicio remarks,

these mathematical subtleties do very well in the abstract, but they do not work out when applied to sensible and physical matters. (Ibid., p. 203)

And later he complains—in a manner that would surely have been approved by Plato himself, perhaps even more than Simplicio's own acknowledged master, Aristotle—that "it is the imperfection of matter which prevents things taken concretely from corresponding to those considered in the abstract" (Ibid., p. 207). Salviati replies that

the mathematical scientist, when he wants to recognize in the concrete the effects which he has proved in the abstract, must deduct the material hindrances, and if he is able to do so, I assure you that things are in no less agreement than arithmetical computations. The errors, then, lie not in the abstractness or concreteness, not in geometry or physics, but in a calculator who does not know how to make a true accounting. (Ibid., pp. 207–8)

Although this passage is not completely unambiguous ("*if* he is able to do so"), the strong suggestion is that nature itself is perfectly determinate, and that it is only our ignorance or incapacity that detracts from the precision of mathematical calculation.

Yet Galileo's statements do not always bear out this interpretation: sometimes he seems to hold that there *is* an inherent indeterminacy of nature which prevents a complete and precise scientific account even "in principle":

> As to the perturbation arising from the resistance of the medium this is more considerable and does not, on account of its manifold forms, submit to fixed laws and exact description. Thus if we consider only the resistance which the air offers to the motions studied by us, we shall see that it disturbs them all and disturbs them in an infinite variety of ways corresponding to the infinite variety in the form, weight, and velocity of the projectiles. . . . Of these properties of weight, of velocity, and also of form, infinite in number, it is impossible to give any exact description; hence, in order to handle this matter in a scientific way, it is necessary to cut loose from all these difficulties; and having discovered and demonstrated the theorems, in the case of no resistance, to use them and apply them with such limitations as experience will teach. (*Two New Sciences*, p. 242)

On the view discussed in the preceding paragraph, "abstraction" or "idealization" (or "thought-experiment") is introduced as a simplifying device which is always capable, in principle, of being made more accurate: by reintroducing into our calculations other factors initially omitted (like friction and air resistance), it is always possible to approximate more and more closely, in our mathematical treatment, to a complete and precise account of the physical situation in its full complexity. On the view suggested by the quotation just given, however, "idealizations," and so forth, are utilized *just because*, beyond a certain point, *no* more complete and accurate account *can* be given. Rather, we simply have to learn to apply our mathematical idealizations "with such limitations as experience will teach"; those limitations themselves—those deviations from our theorems —are not describable in mathematical (or any other) terms

that allow their reintroduction into our calculations to make
our treatment more precise.

As on so many issues, so also on the present one, concerning the limits (if any) of mathematical treatment of nature,
it appears that Galileo's position was not clearly formulated,
and probably he was not even fully cognizant of the issue.
And it seems best to leave the matter at that, rather than to
try to impose an artificial consistency, whether "Platonic"
or "modern," on his thought. Kepler was far more explicit
about the mathematical determinacy of nature, even though
to our minds (and undoubtedly also to Galileo's) his views
were so tinged with mysticism as to appear quaintly pre-
scientific. Descartes was even more explicit, and went much
further in attempting to provide a rational foundation for
the belief that mathematics—specifically, geometry—was
both *necessary* and *sufficient* for a complete and precise
account of physical nature.[4]

The importance of this shift cannot be overemphasized.
Both Plato and Aristotle agreed that mathematics was inadequate to give a complete and precise account of physical
nature, though they disagreed as to the reasons. For Aristotle, mathematics was a mere abstraction, and furthermore
had to do only with accidents, so that an understanding of
essences—the proper goal of science—could not be obtained
through it. For Plato, although mathematics did give us
what understanding of nature could be obtained,[5] nevertheless it could not give a complete and precise understanding,
even in principle (even to a Laplacian Supreme Intelligence), because physical nature has built into it an inherent
and irremovable unintelligibility.

Hence Koyré's attempt to contrast the "Aristotelian" with
the "Platonic" view of the role of mathematics in the interpretation of nature, and to interpret the scientific revolution of Galileo as a Platonic reaction against Aristotelianism, fails, because he has not recognized a crucial point on
which the two Greeks agreed, and on which they were
opposed at least to the mainstream of classical modern
physics. Thus Koyré's attempts to characterize the distinction between Platonism and Aristotelianism often fail, as in
the following instance in which Koyré claims Simplicio to
be expressing the heart of the Aristotelian doctrine as op-

posed both to the Platonic and the modern scientific (or Galilean) viewpoints.

"All these mathematical subtleties," explains Simplicio, "are true in *abstracto*. But applied to sensible and physical matter, they do not work." In real nature there are no circles, no triangles, no straight lines. Therefore it is useless to learn the language of mathematical figures: the book of Nature, in spite of Galileo and Plato, is not written in them. (Koyré, "Galileo and Plato," in Wiener and Noland, p. 170)

But a Platonist, too, could agree that in real nature there are no *perfect* circles, triangles, or straight lines, and that therefore calculations with them will not apply with perfect precision to sensible and physical matter. Again, Koyré tells us:

Galileo, in the margin of [*Two Chief World Systems*] sums up the discussion and formulates the real meaning of the Aristotelian: "In natural demonstrations," says he, "one must not seek mathematical exactitude."
One must not. Why? Because it is impossible. Because the nature of physical being is qualitative and vague. (Ibid., p. 169)

But again—except perhaps for calling the nature of physical being "qualitative"—such a view could also have been maintained by a Platonist.[6] And in the case of both this and the preceding quotation, Aristotle and Plato, far from contradicting one another, would have been in agreement (though on the basis of different reasons) in opposing the "Laplacian" attitude of classical modern physics.

But the defects of Koyré's interpretation of science and history go deeper than this failure to come to grips with the relations between Plato, Aristotle, and classical modern science; for he is also hampered by conceptual confusions. Again and again throughout his writings he expresses his belief in a sharp distinction (questioned severely by many philosophers of science) between "theory" and "fact":

It is impossible in practice to produce a plane surface which is truly plane; or to make a spherical surface which is so in reality. Perfectly rigid bodies do not, and cannot, exist *in rerum natura*; nor can perfectly elastic bodies; and it is not possible to make an absolutely correct measurement. Perfection is not of this world; no doubt we can approach it, but we cannot attain it. Between empirical fact and theoretical concept there remains, and will always remain, a gap that cannot be bridged. (*Metaphysics and Measurement*, p. 45)

(How Koyré's own Platonic leanings come through in these remarks!)

Furthermore, he constantly derogates all but the most direct sorts of empirical tests of theoretical ideas; empirical approximations and "limiting-case" arguments are, to his mind, not to be trusted.[7] ("Galileo's argument [regarding the speed of falling bodies in *Two New Sciences*] is thus put forward as a kind of progression to the limiting case. . . . Of course, this proof is not satisfactory logically" [*Metaphysics and Measurement*, p. 57].)

Seeing, therefore, no possibility of direct or accurate test and measurement of basic theoretical ideas (which can never be fully exemplified in "fact"), Koyré concludes that those ideas must be "prior" to experiment or observation. Thus he claims that the principle of inertia, not being susceptible of any direct test (no body ever being absolutely free of external influences, or capable of being followed in its motion forever), and derogating any indirect test (like a process of successive approximations to freedom from external influences), he concludes that the principle must be obtained prior to experience. And from this step he goes on to conclude that it must be *a priori*, that is, a conclusion drawn from reason, innate in our minds, independent of experience. It is thus not only for Galileo, but also for Koyré himself, that "Good physics is made *a priori*. Theory precedes fact" (*Metaphysics and Measurement*, p. 13).

But even if the principle of inertia (for example) were, and could not be otherwise than, prior to experience, it would not therefore necessarily be a product of "reason," in the sense of having been innate in the mind or discoverable independently of sensory experience. According to one modern version of empiricism, "hypotheses" or "conjectures" are proposed, and *then* tested against experience for verification or falsification (rather than, as with a more traditional version of empiricism, being obtained *from* experiences which were prior to their proposal). According to this "hypothetico-deductive" doctrine, it does not matter *what* the source of the hypotheses might be—though no empiricist would admit that they are products of pure reason. The important point, for this version of empiricism, is that a hypothesis can be advanced prior to experimental testing, and still not be *"a priori"* or a product of "pure reason." And *everything in Koyré's arguments concerning the priority of "theory" to "fact" is compatible with such an empiricist interpretation.*

This is not to say, however, that the "hypothetico-deductive" interpretation of scientific procedure is a magic solution to the problem of understanding the scientific revolution. On the contrary, it suffers from a major defect: in claiming that the *source* of hypotheses is irrelevant to the understanding of science (since such hypotheses can be suggested in the most irrational ways), it ignores the fact that there *are* patterns of reasoning in the construction or discovery (as well as in the ultimate acceptance or rejection) of scientific hypotheses or theories, and that a great deal of illumination of the scientific enterprise can be attained by examining them.[8] Such hypotheses or theories may not be discoveries of pure *reason*, independent of all experience; but the processes of arriving at them are not therefore necessarily unreason*able*, given the ideas, problems, and techniques available at the time they are proposed.

We can see such patterns of reasonable development illustrated in the evolution of Galileo's thought as discussed in this book. Thus, for all the scantiness and difficulty of interpretation of the historical record, we have seen Galileo begin, in *On Motion*, with an attempt to formulate a synthesis of certain traditional views. It was a synthesis which seems a most reasonable one to have attempted, applying as it did the Archimedean analysis of bodies in a fluid medium to the Aristotelian view of the sublunar domain as consisting of layers (now, in Galileo's interpretation, "media") of fire, air, water, and earth, through which bodies fell or rose in "natural" motion; for by that synthesis, Galileo was able to deal with certain problems concerning such motion. And in order to overcome a difficulty (namely, the question of the role of acceleration in such naturally rising or falling motion), he appended to this synthesis certain facets of one version of the medieval Impetus Theory. Having formulated this view, he became convinced of its incorrectness and began to arrive at new views. The considerations that led him to these changes are historically unclear; but whatever the true reasons, we have been able to outline the major possibilities that may have played a role.

On becoming convinced, through his telescopic observations, of the truth of Copernicanism, Galileo began in his characteristic way to attempt to integrate his mechanical ideas with that astronomical doctrine into a general synthetic view. The key to the synthesis he found in assigning a fundamental role to circular motion not only in the heavens (to which Aristotle had confined it), but also in the terrestrial realm. But in thus utilizing the traditional circle as a basis for his integrated views, he tried—again characteristically—to find a deeper, more consistent, and less arbitrary foundation for it. This foundation lay, for Galileo, in the view that the orderliness of the universe (which in turn he deduced from the perfection of the universe[9]) implies the fundamental and exclusive role of circular motion in nature: orderliness, consisting in preservation of proper positional arrangement, requires that only rest, rotation in place, or revolution around a central point be natural to bodies.

It is possible that Galileo believed his assumption about the nature of orderliness—which he accepted as a necessary truth—to be a revelation of pure reason rather than a disclosure of experience; but its being a necessary truth is also perfectly compatible with Aristotle's view that such truths can be abstracted from sensory observation. But even if he did believe, with Plato, that some truths (including this one) are discovered by reason, the particular proposition in question—the principle of order—is not exclusively Platonic, and is so far from being anti-Aristotelian that it was accepted by Aristotle himself as a foundation-stone of his own philosophy.

But whatever the method by which he believed himself to have arrived at his principle of order, and whether or not the argument is valid by which he deduced from it the further proposition that circular motion and only circular motion is natural, Galileo erred in believing his principle of order to be a necessary truth. What he did not realize is that the conception of order as positional arrangement, which he took over unquestioningly from Aristotle, is not necessarily the *only* possible conception of order. On the contrary, there are significant alternatives—including the one that was ultimately to be adopted by science, namely the view that the universe is "ordered" in the sense that things operate, and events occur, in accordance with laws which hold independently of time or place. On that conception of order, occupying a definite location, or even remaining at rest in whatever location (or at least remaining in the immediate vicinity of that location by rotating or revolving) is wholly irrelevant to the concept of an ordered universe. The Aristotelian-Galilean conception of orderliness, far from being a necessary truth, is completely arbitrary.

Galileo was in error on yet another point with regard to the circularity thesis: whereas he considered it logically inseparable from Copernicanism, Newton was to establish conclusively, through his first two laws of motion and law of gravitation, that Copernicanism is perfectly compatible with a denial of the fundamental role of circles. But this has important consequences: for if circularity and Copernicanism are thus logically separable, then the latter is also independent of the purely logical or "rationalistic" arguments by which the naturalness of circular motion was deduced from the principle of order. The observational evidence for Copernicanism—which, after all, was decisive in finally convincing Galileo of the truth of that doctrine—could remain.

Observation certainly played an important part in the development of Galileo's mature thought. And while the historical evidence is, at least as yet, inadequate to decide the extent to which experiments (for example, with inclined planes and pendulums) played a role in the development of his Paduan mechanics, we have found no reason to doubt that they *could* have been important in his achievement and acceptance of some central mathematical relationships, particularly concerning falling bodies. On the other hand, our study does not bear out the simplistic empiricism of Mach, according to which Galileo broke completely with an un-scientific past, developing entirely new concepts and methods without any preconceptions whatever, solely on the basis of observation of "facts." On the contrary, as we have seen, Galileo's thought evolved within a broad and rich framework of traditional ideas, some of which he accepted without question, as necessary truths which served as bases of purely logical arguments which he was willing to trust more confidently than the evidence of his senses.

Still less is it possible to accept the view that Galileo's thought broke completely with the past by providing an entirely new framework or "paradigm" of thought, completely incommensurable with the past, dealing with entirely new problems, using entirely new standards. Galileo's genius departs from an acceptance of a multitude of older ideas, and attempts to integrate them into a coherent whole, while pushing certain of those ideas more deeply than had been done before. His original, and in many respects lasting, inspiration came from the mathematics of Archimedes, applied to essentially Aristotelian and medieval problems in an essentially Aristotelian universe. But it was the geometrical success—and, still more, the physical promise—of Copernicanism, bolstered by the observational evidence of the telescope, that became the decisive influence after 1610; and into the context of that astronomical view, like a master tailor, he wove a host of older ideas, such as the Aristotelian idea of order and the central role of circular motion (which, however, he applied and extended in ways that had not been done before). In Galileo, at least, creativity and originality depart not from rejection and complete replacement but from reorganization and deepening.

But Galileo's work is not mere eclecticism either: the synthesis brought about by genius is not a merely passive process; on the contrary, it is intellectually creative. In the course of integrating and extending the old, he portrayed, through his literary and logical talents, a picture of the universe which, though compounded of the past, was in its totality very unlike anything that had gone before. That picture in turn would be greatly altered during the succeeding century. Nevertheless, it provided a background of ideas and problems on which the future could build, the shoulders of a giant on which later thinkers could climb.

In addition to the general Copernican picture it advocated, and the integration of previously known correct mechanical ideas and relationships, Galileo's thought also included specific ideas which were completely new. Among the most important of these were: his telescopic discoveries; his discovery of the fact that (ignoring air resistance) all bodies, regardless of composition, shape, or any other individual peculiarities, fall at the same rate; and his (and Cavalieri's) discovery of the fact that the path of a projectile is an arc of a parabola. Galileo was ambiguous in his acceptance of the latter result: though the deduction, like some of his other work, stood on the brink of the principle of inertia, he was unable to accept it as more than approximate. And it is one of the ironies of history, and perhaps of creative human thought in general, that it was his commitment to Copernicanism, or rather his mistaken but perfectly understandable notion that that view was logically tied to the central role of circular motion in the universe, that prevented him from accepting it as completely accurate. Nevertheless, even here, where he himself could not enter the promised land, Galileo made it easier for others to do so: for once the technique of decomposing the path of a projectile into two rectilinear components became established (as it did among such Galilean disciples as Cavalieri and Baliani),[10] one of the final obstacles on the road to the principle of inertia and a truly "modern" science had been removed.

$\mathcal{N}otes$

1. Galileo and the Interpretation of Science

1. For further details about the life of Galileo, see Geymonat, *Galileo Galilei*; de Santillana, *The Crime of Galileo*; and Drake, *Galileo Studies*.

2. The Intellectual Background

1. Strictly speaking, Forms correspond to "concepts," or to single terms in a sentence, and so are not true or false (which are properties of sentences or propositions). But relations between Forms correspond to "propositions," and can therefore be legitimately referred to as "truths." This distinction is, however, unimportant for our purposes, and I have not bothered to make it explicitly in the text.

2. There is a question, passed over here, as to whether the Receptacle is properly thought of as Non-Being, or whether it should be viewed as disorder, Chaos, or, indeed, whether there is any difference between Non-Being and Chaos in Plato.

3. Some higher forms, however—for example, Prime Movers—exist apart from matter.

4. There is serious question as to whether the concept of prime matter is really to be found in Aristotle. However, since the Medieval philosophers did believe that notion to be an integral part of Aristotelian philosophy, I have chosen to take their interpretation, since the "Aristotelian" background with which we are concerned here is theirs.

5. Moody says, "In the second chapter of book IV of the *De Caelo* Aristotle states that of two bodies of the same composition or density, the larger one will fall faster than the smaller. Aside from the fact that Aristotle is not considering the case of bodies falling in a non-resistant vacuum, this statement is offered only as a dialectical premise in the course of Aristotle's argument against those who assumed an internal void as cause of

differences in density and rarity of bodies; hence it is highly questionable whether this view can be legitimately ascribed to Aristotle" (Moody, "Galileo and Avempace," in Wiener and Noland, eds., *Roots of Scientific Thought*, p. 191). The very number of passages cited by us here makes it clear that there is no basis for Moody's skepticism as to whether Aristotle really believed seriously that heavier bodies fall faster than light ones.

6. Strictly speaking, if it is distinct from what changes.

7. Even in a finite, walled universe, the *tendency* of bodies might be to move in straight lines forever; they are simply prevented from doing so by the walls. Thus Koyré is wrong in asserting that "the law of inertia implies an infinite world" (Koyré, *Newtonian Studies*, p. 67).

8. That is, antiperistasis alone would require all violent motion to be instantaneous.

9. It is true that the sentence immediately following the passage quoted here suggests that iron *does* receive more impetus than wood: "Now in a dense and heavy body, other things being equal, there is more of prime matter than in a rare and light one. Hence a dense and heavy body receives more of that impetus and more intensely, just as iron can receive more calidity [heat] than wood or water of the same quantity" (Clagett, p. 535). However, the analogy with heat shows that the interpretation given here is correct: just as iron *can* receive more heat than wood, though it *need* not, so also with impetus.

10. Aristotle continues, "And the natural movement of a body may be helped on in the same way." This is often taken as an attempt to explain the acceleration of naturally falling or rising bodies as the result of a violent force superimposed on the constant natural tendency. However, this solution is not clearly satisfactory: for the superimposed force should, on Aristotelian principles, only produce a *constant* added increment of speed.

11. For a more detailed discussion of these points, see my "Scientific Theories and Their Domains," in F. Suppe, ed., *The Nature of Scientific Theories* (Urbana: University of Illinois Press, 1972).

3. The Early Development of Galileo's Thought

1. All pre-Galilean discussions (and also Galileo's in *On Motion*) seem to have considered specific features of the body to be relevant to its behavior in fall.

2. Medieval "internal resistance" views were actually quite varied. For example, another such view, not discussed here, was that the internal resistance is due to a conflict between the

natural tendencies of the elements composing the (mixed) body. See E. Grant, *Physical Science in the Middle Ages*, pp. 44 ff.

3. In his article, "Galileo's Use of Experiment as a Tool of Investigation," Thomas Settle rests much of his argument on the claim that Galileo abandoned the ideas of *On Motion* because he could find "no clear experimental instance in which a freely moving body had lost its retarding impressed power, and was proceeding at a uniform speed" (McMullin, *Galileo*, p. 320). McMullin repeats this incorrect claim that Galileo "had been entirely unable to find direct evidence in its support" (ibid., p. 11).

4. After consultation with Professor W. R. Shea, to whom I am indebted for many valuable suggestions regarding this book, I have altered Drake's translation in certain respects. I have translated *"accidenti"* as "accidents," rather than, as Drake does, "phenomena," in order to avoid the empiricist bias introduced by the latter word. Where Drake has Galileo saying, "I am reduced to a proposition which has much of the natural and the evident," I have used, "I settled on a proposition which seemed quite natural and obvious." It should be noted that the phrase "the accidents observed by me" does not necessarily have any empiricist implications. Settle's translation (in McMullin, *Galileo*, p. 318) conveys the suggestion that Galileo accepted the $v \propto s$ relationship as satisfying his demand for indubitability, a suggestion which is not borne out by the text.

5. It is very unclear what Drake means in suggesting that while there is nothing like what some writers refer to as an inductive rule by which the law was arrived at, it might have been arrived at "indirectly." Is he proposing that some very weak sort of logical rule is involved?

6. Even if Galileo could not have made such observations with an accuracy that would have brought out the odd-number rule, there is an alternative possibility by which he might have arrived at the law: he might have known the Merton Rule, and perhaps also the times-squared and odd-number rules, but had not accepted them; but then his inclined-plane experiments, however rough, might have been close enough to the predictions of those laws to have made him accept them, and even perhaps refine (or fudge) his measurements in accordance with them.

In a paper which appeared too late for discussion in this book ("Galileo's Discovery of the Law of Free Fall"), Stillman Drake, on the basis of a hitherto unexamined document, presents an ingenious new interpretation of Galileo's discovery, according to which it was arrived at "through a combination of error, good luck, persistence and mathematical ingenuity." He also argues that, properly interpreted, the assumption from which Galileo deduces the times-squared law is not incorrect.

4. Galileo and the Principle of Inertia

1. The idea of a common "paradigm" as defining and unifying a "tradition" in science is developed in Kuhn, *The Structure of Scientific Revolutions*.

2. Galileo's argument is invalid unless he assumes that something is eternal *if and only if* it is natural. However, as we saw earlier, the Aristotelian tradition maintained that natural motions with specific *termini* could be noneternal.

3. See, for example, Drake in *Galileo Studies*.

4. For a discussion of Planck's work, see M. J. Klein, "Max Planck and the Beginnings of Quantum Theory" and "Planck, Entropy, and Quanta, 1901–1906."

5. In his early article, "Galileo and Plato" (1943), Koyré maintained that the principle of inertia "implicitly pervades Galilean physics" (Wiener and Noland, p. 150). However, in other writings, Koyré held that Galileo did not achieve the full principle of inertia, but had only a principle of "circular inertia."

6. Drake does try to argue that Galileo was clearer than is often supposed about other aspects of the inertial principle also. He tries, for example, to dissociate Galileo's reliance on circular motion from the "core" of the inertial principle: "He seems always to have continued to associate the phenomena of inertia and of conservation of rotatory motion, which has led most historians to believe that Galileo's inertia had a circular quality. In my opinion, the association had quite another basis; namely, the linkage in Galileo's mind of these two phenomena by the unifying concept of a 'neutral' motion which had first led him to an inertial principle" (Drake, *Galileo Studies*, p. 251). It is not clear, however, how this is supposed to prove that, for Galileo, circular motion was *not* part of Galileo's concept of inertia. On the contrary, it seems to support the view of those historians who claim that "Galileo's inertia had a circular quality."

5. Reason and Experience in Galileo's Thought

1. Strictly speaking, the debate as to whether science could give a complete account of nature continued well beyond the seventeenth century, though in a different guise from that connected here with Platonism. The major eighteenth century controversy was between the *Deists*, who maintained that God at

the creation had embodied in the world laws so perfect that his interference in the universe was thenceforth unnecessary (as a perfect watch never needs to be taken back to the watchmaker for repairs), and the *Theists*, who maintained that God must periodically intervene in the workings of nature to preserve observance of the laws he had embodied there.

The contrast we have made between Plato and classical modern science should not lead anyone to assert that Plato anticipated the "indeterminacy" propounded by quantum theory; for the latter indeterminacy is itself expressible in the form of a set of precise mathematical relationships ("Heisenberg's principle"), an idea completely foreign to Plato's thought.

2. "Necessity" is here opposed to "Reason." For further details, see my "Descartes and Plato," which is a reply to Koyré's "Galileo and Plato."

3. This passage, however, although it clearly asserts that geometry is *necessary* for an understanding of physical nature, is not clear as to whether it is also *sufficient*. (We are told that one must *first* learn to comprehend the language of mathematics; but must one *then* go on to learn some further language before understanding of nature can be achieved?) For Descartes, mathematics (geometry) is clearly and explicitly asserted to be both necessary and sufficient for an understanding of material substance (whose essence is extendedness).

4. It should be understood, however, that the conceptions of "geometry" held by Galileo, Kepler, and Descartes were not identical. Galileo was not very explicit as to what was involved in "geometry"; Kepler's conception, at least insofar as application to the physical world was concerned, was limited to "constructible" (by ruler-and-compass operations) figures; he completely ignored the new developments in algebra, primarily introduced by Vieta, which removed any excuse for such restriction. Descartes, making use of those developments in his creation of analytic geometry, had a wider conception, though it was still limited in ways which were serious not only from the viewpoint of later pure mathematics (restriction to analytic curves), but also from that of consequences for his own program for physics (there was no way of dealing with "motion," and therefore, in the Cartesian philosophy, with distinctions of individuals, in purely geometrical terms; and although a mathematical treatment of motion was made possible by the invention of the calculus, a genuinely Cartesian treatment became possible only in the nineteenth century, with the work of Riemann).

5. The same question, however, arises in regard to Plato as we raised in note 3 of this chapter: is geometry sufficient, or merely necessary, for whatever understanding of physical nature can be obtained?

6. It appears that, for Plato, the elements consisted not only of geometrical shapes, but also of "powers," so that geometry could be only necessary, but not also sufficient, for understanding physical entities. See Cornford, *Plato's Cosmology*, p. 205.

7. For a detailed analysis of the role of "idealizations" and other such "conceptual devices" in science, see my "Notes Toward a Post-Positivistic Interpretation of Science," especially part II.

8. The failure of the hypothetico-deductive view to give any account of, or even to admit the existence of, any rationale of hypothesis development, is shared by the view that fundamental scientific hypotheses or theories are matters of purely arbitrary stipulation. (As if one were to say, "We will henceforth agree by convention—rather than on the basis of any evidence or reason— to accept the principle of inertia.") On such a view, scientific revolutions are simply changes of basic conventions, with all the arbitrariness and relativism that that implies. Such views have been advanced by P. Feyerabend in "Problems of Empiricism" and by T. S. Kuhn in *The Structure of Scientific Revolutions*. For criticism of those views, see my "Meaning and Scientific Change," "The Structure of Scientific Revolutions," and "The Paradigm Concept."

9. In the course of developing even his mature ideas, Galileo did not hesitate to attribute purpose to nature; "perfection" was, indeed, the basis of his claim that the universe is orderly, and that therefore only circular motion is natural, a view which he associated intimately with the Copernicanism which he had come to advocate. And many of his arguments—for instance, about the impossibility of natural rectilinear motion—hinge on the Aristotelian claim that all change in nature requires a terminating form (or final cause). He is also clearly concerned with answering the question "Why?" in the sense of the Aristotelian efficient cause. It is true that in *Two New Sciences* such questions are put into the background; but especially with regard to questions of efficient causation, they are not abandoned, but merely postponed.

> The present does not seem to be the proper time to investigate the cause of the acceleration of natural motion concerning which various opinions have been expressed by various philosophers. . . . Now, all these fantasies, and others too, ought to

be examined; but it is not really worth while. At present it is the purpose of our Author merely to investigate and to demonstrate some of the properties of accelerated motion (whatever the cause of this acceleration may be). (*Two New Sciences*, p. 160)

That Galileo was able to put such questions aside was, of course, an important step (though not original with him), but there seems no warrant for claiming it to have been fundamental to the development of a new science, and still less for claiming that the abandonment of "Why?" questions, at least in the sense of efficient, if not of final, causation and a rigorous limitation to "How?" questions, are essential ingredients of the scientific enterprise.

There are three other main aspects of Galileo's discussions of scientific method which have not been considered in this book: his distinction between methods of "resolution" and "composition"; his distinction between "primary" and "secondary" qualities; and his advocacy of atomism. His discussions of these topics, however, are quite superficial, especially when compared to similar discussions by other writers; their importance (and especially that of the discussions of method in *The Assayer*) for understanding Galileo and his work seems to me to have been greatly exaggerated.

10. We must not neglect the possibility here that the rectilinear impetus theory, say in the form presented by Benedetti, might also have influenced these students of Galileo; they may also have been impressed by Galileo's discussion of tangential tendencies conveyed by a rotating body, in *Two Chief World Systems*, pages 174–95.

Bibliography

Antonio Favaro's National Edition of Galileo's *Opere* (Florence, 1890–1909) is the standard collection of Galileo's works. An indispensable guide to Galilean literature is the "Bibliographia Galileiana, 1940–1964," compiled under the direction of Ernan McMullin and included as Appendix A to his *Galileo: Man of Science*. The comments at the beginning of that appendix contain references to other such bibliographies. The following works are either discussed directly in the present book or especially useful in connection with topics discussed therein.

Archimedes. *Works*. Edited by T. L. Heath. New York: Dover, 1897.

Aristotle. *Works*. Vol. 1. Oxford: Clarendon, 1968. (Relevant contents: *Categories* and *Posterior Analytics*.)

Aristotle. *Works*. Vol. 2. Oxford: Clarendon, 1966. (Contains *Physics, On the Heavens*, and *On Generation and Corruption*.)

Butterfield, H. *The Origins of Modern Science, 1300–1800*. New York: Macmillan, 1958.

Clagett, M. *The Science of Mechanics in the Middle Ages*. Madison: University of Wisconsin Press, 1959.

Clavelin, M. *La philosophie naturelle de Galilée*. Paris: Librairie Armand Colin, 1968.

Cohen, I. B. *The Birth of a New Physics*. Garden City, N. Y.: Doubleday, 1960.

Cohen, M. R., and Drabkin, I. E., eds. *A Source Book in Greek Science*. Cambridge: Harvard University Press, 1948.

Cornford, F. M. *Plato's Cosmology*. New York: Liberal Arts Press, 1957. (Plato's *Timaeus* with commentary.)

Crombie, A. C. *Medieval and Early Modern Science*. 2 vols. Garden City, N. Y.: Doubleday, 1959.

Dijksterhuis, E. J. *The Mechanization of the World Picture*. Oxford: Clarendon, 1961.

Dreyer, J. L. E. *A History of Astronomy from Thales to Kepler.* New York: Dover, 1953.

Drake, S. "Galileo and the Law of Inertia." *American Journal of Physics* 32 (1964): 601–8.

——. *Galileo Studies.* Ann Arbor: University of Michigan Press, 1970.

——. "Galileo's Discovery of the Law of Free Fall." *Scientific American* 228, no. 5 (May 1973).

——. "Galileo's 1604 Fragment on Falling Bodies." *British Journal for the History of Science* 4 (1969): 341–58.

Drake, S., and Drabkin, I. E. *Mechanics in Sixteenth-Century Italy.* Madison: University of Wisconsin Press, 1969.

Drake, S., and O'Malley, C. D. *The Controversy on the Comets of 1618.* Philadelphia: University of Pennsylvania Press, 1960. (Works by Galileo, Grassi, Guiducci, and Kepler.)

Duhem, P. *The Aim and Structure of Physical Theory.* Princeton: Princeton University Press, 1954.

Fermi, L., and Bernardini, G. *Galileo and the Scientific Revolution.* New York: Basic Books, 1961. (Contains a translation of *The Little Balance.*)

Feyerabend, P. "Problems of Empiricism." In *Beyond the Edge of Certainty*, edited by R. Colodny. Englewood Cliffs, N. J.: Prentice-Hall, 1965.

Galilei, G. *Dialogue Concerning the Two Chief World Systems.* Translated by Stillman Drake. Berkeley: University of California Press, 1962.

——. *Dialogue on the Great World Systems.* Translated by Giorgio de Santillana. Chicago: University of Chicago Press, 1957.

——. *Dialogues Concerning Two New Sciences.* New York: Dover, 1914.

——. *Discourse on Bodies in Water.* Urbana: University of Illinois Press, 1960.

——. *Discoveries and Opinions.* Garden City, N. Y.: Doubleday, 1957.

——. *On Motion and Mechanics.* Madison: University of Wisconsin Press, 1960.

Geymonat, L. *Galileo Galilei: A Biography and Inquiry into His Philosophy of Science.* New York: McGraw-Hill, 1965.

Golino, C., ed. *Galileo Reappraised.* Berkeley: University of California Press, 1966.

Grant, E. *Physical Science in the Middle Ages.* New York: Wiley, 1971.

Hall, A. R. *From Galileo to Newton, 1630–1720.* New York: Harper and Row, 1963.

Klein, M. J. "Max Planck and the Beginnings of Quantum Theory." *Archive for History of the Exact Sciences* 1 (1962): 459 ff.

———. "Planck, Entropy, and Quanta, 1901–1906." *The Natural Philosopher.* Vol. 1. New York: Blaisdell, 1963. pp. 83–108.

Koyré, A. *A Documentary History of the Problem of Fall from Kepler to Newton.* Philadelphia: American Philosophical Society, 1955.

———. *Etudes Galiléennes.* Paris: Hermann, 1966.

———. *Metaphysics and Measurement.* Cambridge: Harvard University Press, 1968.

———. *Newtonian Studies.* Cambridge: Harvard University Press, 1965.

Kuhn, T. S. *The Copernican Revolution.* Cambridge: Harvard University Press, 1957.

———. *The Structure of Scientific Revolutions.* Chicago: University of Chicago Press, 1970.

Laplace, P. S. de. *A Philosophical Essay on Probabilities.* New York: Dover, 1951.

Mach, E. *The Science of Mechanics.* La Salle, Ill.: Open Court, 1960.

McMullin, E., ed. *Galileo: Man of Science.* New York: Basic Books, 1967.

Santillana, Giorgio de. *The Crime of Galileo.* Chicago: University of Chicago Press, 1955.

Shapere, D. "Copernicanism as a Scientific Revolution." In *Copernicanism Yesterday and Today,* edited by K. A. Strand and A. Beer. New York: Pergamon, 1974.

———. "Descartes and Plato." *Journal of the History of Ideas* (1963): 572–76.

———. "Meaning and Scientific Change." In *Mind and Cosmos: Explorations in the Philosophy of Science,* edited by R. Colodny. Pittsburgh: University of Pittsburgh Press, 1966.

———. "Notes Toward a Post-Positivistic Interpretation of Science." In *The Legacy of Logical Positivism,* edited by P. Achinstein and S. Barker. Baltimore: Johns Hopkins University Press, 1969.

———. "The Paradigm Concept." *Science* 172 (14 May 1971): 706–9.

———. "Scientific Theories and Their Domains." In *The Nature of Scientific Theory,* edited by F. Suppe. Urbana: University of Illinois Press, 1974.

——. "The Structure of Scientific Revolutions. *Philosophical Review*, 1964, pp. 383–94.

Shea, W. R. *Galileo's Intellectual Revolution*. London: Macmillan, 1972.

Wiener, P. P., and Noland, A. *Roots of Scientific Thought*. New York: Basic Books, 1957. (Includes articles by Randall, Koyré, and Moody.)

Index

Albert of Saxony, 58
Antiperistasis ("mutual replacement" theory), 46–48, 148
Archimedes, 11, 15, 22, 72–73, 78, 119, 141
Aristotle (and Aristotelianism), 6–8, 12, 15–16, 19, 22–23, 28–49, 51, 53, 55–56, 59–67, 69–72, 74, 78, 85, 87–93, 99–101, 106, 108–9, 111–12, 114–16, 129, 131, 136, 138–39, 141–44, 147–48, 150–52; change, 30–31; Christianity, 32–33; on comets, 16; compared with Buridan's impetus theory, 55–56; concept of order of universe, 87–88, 142–44; essence vs. accident, 28–29; five elements, 34–36; form vs. matter, 28; four causes, 31; heaviness and lightness, 35–38, 40–41, 69, 73–74; infinity, 29–30; laws of motion, 36–42, 62; on mathematics, 129, 137–39; nature, 31–32, 70–71; observation, 28–29, 43–45; place, 33; potentiality vs. actuality, 29–30; prime matter, 29, 36, 47, 55–56; and Ptolemaic system, 66; structure of the universe, 33–35, 65; theory of violent motion, 39–42, 45–49, 56; void, 42–43

Avempace, 73, 122

Barberini, Maffeo. *See* Urban VIII
Bellarmine, Robert, 17–18, 20
Benedetti, Giambattista, 52, 72–73, 76–77, 153
Bradwardine, Thomas, 56–57
Brahe, Tycho, 15–16, 22, 65. *See also* Tychonic system
Buridan, John, 48–56, 77, 124
Butterfield, Herbert, 63

Castelli, Benedetto, 16, 123
Cavalieri, Buonaventura, 106–7, 145
Clagett, Marshall, 48–51
Cohen, Morris, 48
Continuity, Principle of, 94, 96, 111
Copernicus (and Copernicanism), 4, 13–15, 17, 19–20, 22, 64–68, 101–2, 105, 107, 112–13, 119–20, 126–27, 142–45, 152
Crucial experiments (comments on), 63

Deism, 150
Descartes, René, 122–23, 138, 151
Dijksterhuis, E., 78
Dominicans, 16–17, 19
Drabkin, I., 48, 77